Also by Mark Myers

A Smarter Way to Learn HTML & CSS

Learn it faster.
Remember it longer.

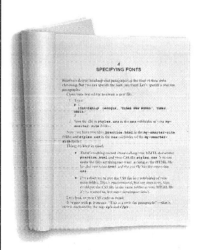

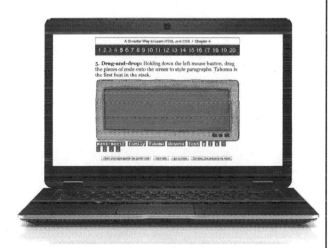

1 Read a 10-minute chapter of this book to get each concept.

2 Make the knowledge stick. Do the chapter's free interactive exercises at ASmarterWayToLearn.com.

Mark Myers

A Smarter Way to Learn JavaScript

Mark Myers

Contents

Learn it faster.
Remember it longer.

If you embrace this method of learning, you'll get the hang of HTML and CSS in less time than you might expect. And the knowledge will stick.

You'll catch onto concepts quickly.

You'll be less bored, and might even be excited. You'll certainly be motivated.

You'll feel confident instead of frustrated.

You'll remember the lessons long after you close the book.

Is all this too much for a book to promise? Yes, it is. Yet I can make these promises and keep them, because this isn't just a book. It's a book plus 1,800 interactive online exercises. I've done my best to write each chapter so it's easy for anyone to understand, but it's the exercises that are going to turn you into a real HTML coder.

Cognitive research shows that reading alone doesn't buy you much long-term retention. Even if you read a book a second or even a third time, things won't improve much, according to research.

And forget highlighting or underlining. Marking up a book gives us the illusion that we're engaging with the material, but studies show that it's an exercise in self-deception. It doesn't matter how much yellow you paint on the pages, or how many times you review the highlighted material. By the time you get to Chapter 50, you'll have forgotten most of what you highlighted in Chapter 1.

This all changes if you read less and do more—if you read a short passage and then immediately put it into practice. Washington University researchers say that being asked to retrieve information increases long-term retention by four hundred percent. That may seem implausible, but by the time you finish this book, I think you'll believe it.

Practice also makes learning more interesting.

Trying to absorb long passages of technical material puts you to sleep and kills your motivation. Ten minutes of reading followed by twenty minutes of challenging practice keeps you awake and spurs you on.

And it keeps you honest.

If you *only* read, it's easy to kid yourself that you're learning more than you are. But when you're challenged to produce the goods, there's a moment of truth. You *know* that you know—or that you don't. When you find out that you're a little shaky on this point or that, you can review the material, then re-do the exercise. That's all it takes to master this book from beginning to end.

I've talked with many readers who say they thought they had a problem understanding technical concepts. But what looked like a comprehension problem was really a retention problem. If you get to Chapter 50 and everything you studied in Chapter 1 has faded from memory, how can you understand Chapter 50, which depends on your knowing Chapter 1 cold? The read-then-practice approach embeds the concepts of each chapter in your long-term memory, so you're prepared to tackle material in later chapters that builds on top of those concepts. When you're able to remember what you read, you'll find that you learn HTML and CSS quite readily.

I hope you enjoy this learning approach. And then I hope you go on to set the Internet on fire with some terrific webpages.

How to use this book

This isn't a book quite like any you've ever owned before, so a brief user manual might be helpful.

- **Brush up on HTML and CSS before you start the second half of the book.** The first half offers an introduction to fundamental programming concepts. The second half shows you how to manipulate HTML and CSS. If you don't know any HTML and CSS, the second half won't make much sense to you. My recommendation: Read (and practice with) my book, *A Smarter Way to Learn HTML & CSS*, before you get too far along in this book.

- **Study, practice, then rest.** If you're intent on mastering the fundamentals of JavaScript, as opposed to just getting a feel for the language, work with this book and the online exercises in a 15-to-30-minute session, then take a break. Study a chapter for 5 to 10 minutes. Immediately go to the online link given at the end of each chapter and code for 10 to 20 minutes, practicing the lesson until you've coded everything correctly. Then take a walk.

- **Do the coding exercises on a physical keyboard.** A mobile device can be ideal for reading, but it's no way to code. Very, very few Web developers would attempt to do their work on a phone. The same thing goes for learning to code. Theoretically, most of the interactive exercises could be done on a mobile device. But the idea seems so perverse that I've disabled online practice on tablets, readers, and phones.

- **If you have an authority problem, try to get over it.** When you start doing the exercises, you'll find that I can be a pain about insisting that you get every little detail right. For example, if you indent a line one space instead of two spaces, the program monitoring your work will tell you the code isn't correct, even though it would still run perfectly. Do I insist on having everything just so because I'm a control freak? No, it's because I have to place a limit on harmless maverick behavior in order to automate the exercises. If I were to grant you as much freedom as you might like, creating the algorithms that check your work would be, for me, a project of driverless-car proportions. Besides, learning to write code with fastidious precision helps you learn to pay close attention to details, a fundamental requirement for coding in any language.

- **Subscribe, temporarily, to my formatting biases.** Current code formatting is like seventeenth-century spelling. Everyone does it his own way. There are no universally accepted standards. But the algorithms that check your work when you do the interactive exercises need standards. They can't grant you the latitude that a human teacher could, because, let's face it, they aren't that bright. So I've had to settle on certain conventions. All of the conventions I teach are embraced by a large segment of the coding community, so you'll be in good company. But that doesn't mean you'll be married to my formatting biases forever. When you begin coding projects, you'll soon develop your own opinions or join an organization that has a stylebook. Until then, I'll ask you to make your code look like my code.

The language you're learning here

JavaScript is a programming language created specifically for the Web. Unlike general-purpose languages like C, Python, and Java, it runs only in a Web browser, in partnership with a webpage that displays in the browser. It can't run independently. This means it must always be included in an HTML file (the file that creates webpage), either mixed in with the HTML code or referenced, within the HTML file, through a link to a separate JavaScript file. You'll learn how to link an HTML file and a JavaScript file in Chapter 43.

Since JavaScript is inseparable from HTML and is often used to manipulate it, I recommend that you have some knowledge of HTML and HTML's formatting partner CSS before tackling JavaScript. If you don't know any HTML or CSS, it might be a good idea to put this book aside for a few weeks and start with my "A Smarter Way to Learn HTML & CSS."

1
Alerts

An **alert** is a box that pops up to give the user a message. Here's code for an alert that displays the message "Thanks for your input!"

```
alert("Thanks for your input!");
```

alert is a *keyword*—that is, a word that has special meaning for JavaScript. It means, "Display, in an alert box, the message that follows." Note that **alert** isn't capitalized. If you capitalize it, the script will stop.

The parentheses are a special requirement of JavaScript, one that you'll soon get used to. You'll be typing parentheses over and over again, in all kinds of JavaScript statements.

In coding, the quoted text "Thanks for your input!" is called a *text string* or simply a *string*. The name makes sense: it's a string of characters enclosed in quotes. Outside the coding world, we'd just call it a quotation.

Note that the opening parenthesis is jammed up against the keyword, and the opening quotation mark is hugging the opening parenthesis. Since JavaScript ignores spaces (except in text strings), you could write...

```
alert ( "Thanks for your input!" );
```

But I want you to know the style conventions of JavaScript, so I'll ask you to always omit spaces before and after parentheses.

In English, a careful writer ends every declarative sentence with a period. In scripting, a careful coder ends every statement with a semicolon. (Sometimes complex, paragraph-like statements end with a curly bracket instead of a semicolon. That's something I'll cover in a later chapter.) A semicolon isn't always necessary, but it's easier to end every statement with a semicolon, rather than stop to figure out whether you need one. In this training, I'll ask you to end *every* statement (that doesn't end with a curly bracket) with a semicolon.

Coding Alternatives to Be Aware Of

- Some coders write **window.alert** instead of, simply, **alert**. This is a highly formal but perfectly correct way to write it. Most coders prefer the short form. We'll stick to the short form in this training.

- In the example above, some coders would use single rather than double quotation marks. This is legal, as long as it's a matching pair. But in a case like this, I'll ask you to use double quotation marks.

Find the interactive coding exercises for this chapter at: http://www.ASmarterWayToLearn.com/js/1.html

2
Variables for Strings

Please memorize the following facts.

- My name is Mark.

- My nationality is U.S.

Now that you've memorized my name and nationality, I won't have to repeat them, literally, again. If I say to you, "You probably know other people who have my name," you'll know I'm referring to "Mark."

If I ask you whether my nationality is the same as yours, I won't have to ask, "Is your nationality the same as U.S.?" I'll ask, "Is your nationality the same as my nationality?" You'll remember that when I say "my nationality," I'm referring to "U.S.", and you'll compare your nationality to "U.S.", even though I haven't said "U.S." explicitly.

In these examples, the terms "my name" and "my nationality" work the same way JavaScript variables do. My name is a term that refers to a particular value, "Mark." In the same way, a *variable* is a word that refers to a particular value.

A variable is created when you write **var** (for variable) followed by the name that you choose to give it. It takes on a particular value when you assign the value to it. This is a JavaScript statement that creates the variable **name** and assigns the value "Mark" to it.

```
var name = "Mark";
```

Now the variable **name** refers to the text string "Mark".

Note that it was my choice to call it name. I could have called it **myName**, **xyz**, **lol**, or something else. It's up to me how to name my variables, within limits.

With the string "Mark" assigned to the variable name, my JavaScript code doesn't have to specify "Mark" again. Whenever JavaScript encounters **name**, JavaScript knows that it's a variable that refers to "Mark".

For example, if you ask JavaScript to print **name**, it remembers the value that **name** refers to, and prints...

Mark

The value that a variable refers to can change.

Let's get back to the original examples, the facts I asked you to memorize. These facts can change, and if they do, the terms *my name* and *my nationality* will refer to new values.

I could go to court and change my name to Ace. Then my name is no longer Mark. If I want you to address me correctly, I'll have to tell you that my name is now Ace. After I tell you that, you'll know that my name doesn't refer to the value it used to refer to (Mark), but refers to a new value (Ace).

If I transfer my nationality to U.K., my nationality is no longer U.S. It's U.K. If I want you to know my nationality, I'll have to tell you that it is now U.K. After I tell you that, you'll know that my nationality doesn't refer to the original value, "U.S.", but now refers to a new value.

JavaScript variables can also change.

If I code...

```
var name = "Mark";
```

...**name** refers to "Mark". Then I come along and code the line...

```
name = "Ace";
```

Before I coded the new line, if I asked JavaScript to print **name**, it printed...

Mark

But that was then.

Now if I ask JavaScript to print **name**, it prints...

Ace

A variable can have any number of values, but only one at a time.

You may be wondering why, in the statement above that assigns "Ace" to name, the keyword **var** is missing. It's because the variable was declared earlier, in the original statement that assigned "Mark" to it. Remember, **var** is the keyword that creates a variable—the keyword that declares it. Once a variable has been declared, you don't have to declare it again. You can just assign the new value to it.

You can declare a variable in one statement, leaving it undefined. Then you can assign a value to it in a later statement, without declaring it again.

```
var nationality;
nationality = "U.S.";
```

In the example above, the assignment statement follows the declaration statement immediately. But any amount of code can separate the two statements, as long as the declaration statement comes first. In fact, there's no law that says you have to ever define a variable that you've declared.

JavaScript variable names have no inherent meaning to JavaScript.

In English, words have meaning. You can't use just any word to communicate. I can say, "My name is Mark," but, if I want to be understood, I can't say, "My floogle is Mark." That's nonsense.

But with variables, JavaScript is blind to semantics. You can use just any word (as long as it doesn't break the rules of variable-naming). From JavaScript's point of view...

```
var floogle = "Mark";
```

...is just as good as...

```
var name = "Mark";
```

If you write...

```
var floogle = "Mark";
```

...then ask JavaScript to print **floogle**, JavaScript prints...
    Mark

Within limits, you can name variables anything you want, and JavaScript won't care.

```
var lessonAuthor = "Mark";
var guyWhoKeepsSayingHisOwnName = "Mark";
var x = "Mark";
```

JavaScript's blindness to meaning notwithstanding, when it comes to variable names, you'll want to give your variables meaningful names, because it'll help you and other coders understand your code.

Again, the syntactic difference between variables and text strings is that variables are never enclosed in quotes, and text strings are always enclosed in quotes.

It's always...

```
var lastName = "Smith";
var cityOfOrigin = "New Orleans";
var aussieGreeting = "g'Day";
```

If it's an alphabet letter or word, and it isn't enclosed in quotes, and it isn't a keyword that has special meaning for JavaScript, like **alert**, it's a variable.

If it's some characters enclosed in quotes, it's a text string.

If you haven't noticed, let me point out the spaces between the variable and the equal sign, and between the equal sign and the value.

```
var nickname = "Bub";
```

These spaces are a style choice rather than a legal requirement. But I'll ask you to include them in your code throughout the practice exercises.

In the last chapter you learned to write...

```
alert("Thanks for your input!");
```

When the code executes, a message box displays saying "Thanks for your input!"

But what if you wrote these two statements instead (the line numbers are added automatically by the editing program; they're not part of your code):

```
1 var thanx = "Thanks for your input!";
2 alert(thanx);
```

Instead of placing a text string inside the parentheses of the *alert* statement, the code above assigns the text string to a variable. Then it places the variable, not the string, inside the parentheses. Because JavaScript always substitutes the value for the variable, JavaScript displays—not the variable name **thanx** but the text to which it refers, "Thanks for your input!" That same alert, "Thanks for your input!" displays.

Find the interactive coding exercises for this chapter at http://www.ASmarterWayToLearn.com/js/2.html

3
Variables for Numbers

A string isn't the only thing you can assign to a variable. You can also assign a number.

```
var weight = 150;
```

Having coded the statement above, whenever you write **weight** in your code, JavaScript knows you mean 150. You can use this variable in math calculations.

If you ask JavaScript to add 25 to **weight**...

```
weight + 25
```

...JavaScript, remembering that **weight** refers to 150, will come up with the sum 175.

Unlike a string, a number is not enclosed in quotes. That's how JavaScript knows it's a number that it can do math on and not a text string, like a ZIP code, that it handles as text.

But then, since it's not enclosed in quotes, how does JavaScript know it's not a variable? Well, because a number, or any combination of characters starting with a number, can't be used as a variable name. If it's a number, JavaScript rejects it as a variable. So it must be a number.

If you enclose a number in quotation marks, it's a string. JavaScript can't do addition on it. It can do addition only on numbers not enclosed in quotes.

Now look at this code.

```
1 var originalNum = 23;
2 var newNum = originalNum + 7;
```

In the second statement in the code above, JavaScript substitutes the number 23 when it encounters the variable **originalNum**. It adds 7 to 23. And it assigns the result, 30, to the variable **newNum**.

JavaScript can also handle an expression made up of nothing but variables. For example...

```
1 var originalNum = 23;
2 var numToBeAdded = 7;
3 var newNum = originalNum + numToBeAdded;
```

A variable can be used in calculating its own new value.

```
1 var originalNum = 90;
2 originalNum = originalNum + 10;
```

If you enclose a number in quotation marks and add 7...

```
1 var originalNum = "23";
2 var newNum = originalNum + 7;
```

...it won't work, because JavaScript can't sum a string and a number. JavaScript interprets "23" as a word, not a number. In the second statement, it doesn't add 23 + 7 to total 30. It does something that might surprise you. I'll tell you about this in a subsequent chapter. For now, know that a number enclosed by quotation marks is not a number, but a string, and JavaScript can't do addition on it.

Note that any particular variable name can be the name of a number variable or string variable. From JavaScript's point of view, there's nothing in a name that denotes one kind of variable or another. In fact, a variable can start out as one type of variable, then become another type of variable.

Did you notice what's new in...

```
1 var originalNumber = 23;
2 var newNum = originalNumber + 7;
```

The statement assigns to the variable **newNum** the result of a mathematical operation. The result of this operation, of course, is a number value.

The example mixes a variable and a literal number in a math expression. But you could also use nothing but numbers or nothing but variables. It's all the same to JavaScript.

I've told you that you can't begin a variable name with a number. The statement...

```
var 1stPrimeNumber = 2;
```

...is illegal, thanks to that initial "1" in the variable name.

But you can include numbers in variable names, as long as none of them come first. The statement...

```
var primeNumberThatComes1st = 2;
```

...is legal.

Conveniently, if you specify a number instead of a string as an alert message...

```
alert(144);
```

...or if you specify a variable that represents a number as an alert message...

```
1 var caseQty = 144;
2 alert(caseQty);
```

...JavaScript automatically converts it to a string and displays it.

Find the interactive coding exercises for this chapter at http://www.ASmarterWayToLearn.com/js/3.html

4
Variable Names Legal and Illegal

You've already learned two rules about naming a variable: You can't enclose it in quotation marks. And the name can't be a number or start with a number.

A variable can't be any of JavaScript's *reserved* words or keywords—the special words that act as programming instructions, like **alert** and **var**.

Here's a list of reserved words that can't be used as variable names.

abstract	final	protected
alert	finally	public
as	float	return
boolean	for	short
break	function	static
byte	goto	super
case	if	switch
catch	implements	synchronized
char	import	this
class	in	throw
continue	instanceof	throws
const	int	transient
debugger	interface	true
default	is	try
delete	long	typeof
do	namespace	use
double	native	var
else	new	void
enum	null	volatile
export	package	while
extends	private	with
false		

Here are the rest of the rules:

- A variable name can't contain any spaces.

- A variable name can contain only letters, numbers, dollar signs, and underscores.

- Though a variable name can't be any of JavaScript's keywords, it can contain keywords. For example, userAlert and **myVar** are legal.

- Capital letters are fine, but be careful. Variable names are case sensitive. A **rose** is not a **Rose**. If you assign the string "Floribundas" to the variable rose, and then ask JavaScript for the value assigned to **Rose**, you'll come up empty.

- I teach the camelCase naming convention. Why "camelCase"? Because there is a hump or two (or three) in the middle if the name is formed by more than one word. A camelCase name begins in lower case. If there's more than one word in the name, each subsequent word gets an initial cap, creating a hump. If you form a variable name with only one word, like **response**, there's no hump. It's a camel that's out of food. Please adopt the camelCase convention. It'll make your variable names more readable, and you'll be less likely to get variable names mixed up.

  Examples:

  ```
  userResponse
  userResponseTime
  userResponseTimeLimit
  response
  ```

- Make your variable names descriptive, so it's easier to figure out what your code means when you or someone else comes back to it three weeks or a year from now. Generally, **userName** is better than **x**, and **faveBreed** is better than **favBrd**, though the shorter names are perfectly legal. You do have to balance readability with conciseness, though. **bestSupportingActressInADramaOrComedy** is a model of clarity, but may be too much for most of us to type or read. I'd shorten it.

Find the interactive coding exercises for this chapter at http://www.ASmarterWayToLearn.com/js/4.html

5
Math expressions: Familiar operators

Wherever you can use a number, you can use a math expression. For example, you're familiar with this kind of statement.

```
var popularNumber = 4;
```

But you can also write this.

```
var popularNumber = 2 + 2;
```

You can also write:

```
alert(2 + 2);
```

This displays the message "4" in an alert box.

When it sees a math expression, JavaScript always does the math and delivers the result.

Here's a statement that subtracts 24 from 12, assigning -12 to the variable.

```
var popularNumber = 12 - 24;
```

This one assigns the product of 3 times 12, 36, to the variable.

```
var popularNumber = 3 * 12;
```

This one assigns 12 divided by 4, 3, to the variable.

```
var popularNumber = 12 / 4;
```

In this one, the number 10 is assigned to a variable. Then 200 is added to the variable, and the sum, 210, is assigned to a second variable. As usual, you can mix variables and numbers.

```
1 var num = 10;
2 var popularNumber = num + 200;
```

You can also use nothing but variables.

```
1 var num = 10;
2 var anotherNum = 1;
3 var popularNumber = num + anotherNum;
```

The arithmetic operators I've been using, **+**, **–**, *****, and **/**, are undoubtedly familiar to you. This one may not be:

```
var whatsLeftOver = 10 % 3;
```

% is the *modulus operator*. It doesn't give you the result of dividing one number by another. It gives you the remainder when the division is executed. In the example above, **whatsLeftOver** has a value of 1.

If one number divides evenly into another, the modulus operation returns 0. In the following statement, 0 is assigned to the variable.

```
var whatsLeftOver = 9 % 3;
```

Find the interactive coding exercises for this chapter at http://www.ASmarterWayToLearn.com/js/5.html

6
Math expressions: Unfamiliar operators

Here's a new one:

```
num++;
```

This is a short way of writing...

```
num = num + 1;
```

It increments the variable by 1.
You decrement using minuses instead of pluses.

```
num--;
```

You can use these expressions in an assignment. But now brace yourself, because you're about to encounter the most irksome, counterintuitive bit of JavaScript behavior in this book. Look at this.

```
1 var num = 1;
2 var newNum = num++;
```

It would be logical to assume that both variables get incremented and wind up with a value of 2. But that isn't the case. Only the original variable, **num**, gets incremented. The new variable, **newNum**, gets shortchanged. It winds up with the original variable's value of 1. Strangely, the **++** doesn't apply to it.

Step 1

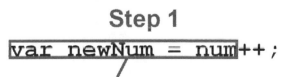

First the new variable is assigned the
value of the original variable.

Step 2

var newNum = num++;

Then the original variable is incremented—
too late for the new variable to benefit.

It's a short way of writing…

```
1 var num = 1;
2 var newNum = num;
3 num++;
```

If you want to increment *both* variables, you must put the pluses *before* the variable, like this:

```
1 var num = 1;
2 var newNum = ++num;
```

Now both **num** and **newNum** wind up with a value of 2.

It's a short way of writing…

```
1 var num = 1;
2 num++;
3 var newNum = num;
```

It works the same way with minuses.

If this seems nuts to you and doesn't seem worth the trouble, just use the pluses in a simple, unconfusing statement, like…

```
num++;
```

…and skip the shorthand for assignments. After all, it isn't that much extra trouble to write…

```
1 var num = 1;
2 num++;
3 var newNum = num;
```

If that's your preference, feel free to skip the exercises that test you on the nutty behavior.

But if you want to master this and you're struggling, I've posted some additional help:

Watch the video at http://player.vimeo.com/video/106125072

Run the code (click the **Run** button) at
http://jsfiddle.net/ASmarterWayToLearn/ubr6jehj/

Find the interactive coding exercises for this chapter at
http://www.ASmarterWayToLearn.com/js/6.html

7
Math expressions: Eliminating ambiguity

Complex arithmetic expressions can pose a problem, one that you may remember from high school algebra. Look at this example and tell me what the value of **totalCost** is.

```
var totalCost = 1 + 3 * 4;
```

The value of **totalCost** varies, depending on the order in which you do the arithmetic. If you begin by adding 1 + 3, then multiply the sum by 4, **totalCost** has the value of 16. But if you go the other way and start by multiplying 3 by 4, then add 1 to the product, you get 13.

In JavaScript as in algebra, the ambiguity is cleared up by precedence rules. As in algebra, the rule that applies here is that multiplication operations are completed before addition operations. So totalCost has the value of 13.

But you don't have to memorize JavaScript's complex precedence rules. You can finesse the issue by using parentheses to eliminate ambiguity. Parentheses override all the built-in precedence rules. They force JavaScript to complete operations enclosed by parentheses before completing any other operations.

When you use parentheses to make your intentions clear to JavaScript, it also makes your code easier to grasp, both for other coders and for you when you're trying to understand your own code a year down the road. In this statement, the parentheses tell JavaScript to first multiply 3 by 4, then add 1. The result: 13.

```
var totalCost = 1 + (3 * 4);
```

If I move the parentheses, the arithmetic is done in a different order. In this next statement, the placement of the parentheses tells JavaScript to first add 1 and 3, then multiply by 4. The result is 16.

```
var totalCost = (1 + 3) * 4;
```

Here's another example.

```
var resultOfComputation = (2 * 4) * 4 + 2;
```

By placing the first multiplication operation inside parentheses, you've told JavaScript to do that operation first. But then what? The order could be..

- Multiply 2 by 4.

- Multiply that product by 4.

- Add 2 to it.

...giving **resultOfComputation** a value of 34.
Or the order could be...

- Multiply 2 by 4.

- Multiply that product by the sum of 4 and 2.

...giving **resultOfComputation** a value of 48.
The solution is more parentheses.
If you want the second multiplication to be done before the 2 is added, write this...

```
resultOfComputation = ((2 * 4) * 4) + 2;
```

But if you want the product of 2 times 4 to be multiplied by the number you get when you total 4 and 2, write this...

```
resultOfComputation = (2 * 4) * (4 + 2);
```

Find the interactive coding exercises for this chapter at http://www.ASmarterWayToLearn.com/js/7.html

8
Concatenating text strings

In Chapter 1 you learned to display a message in an alert, coding it this way.

```
alert("Thanks for your input!");
```

Or you could code it this way.

```
1 var message = "Thanks for your input!";
2 alert(message);
```

But suppose you wanted to personalize a message. In another part of your code you've asked the user for her name and assigned the name that she entered to a variable, **userName**. (You don't know how to do this yet. You'll learn how in a subsequent chapter.)

Now, you want to combine her name with a standard "Thanks" to produce an alert that says, for example, "Thanks, Susan!"

When the user provided her name, we assigned it to the variable **userName**. This is the code.

```
alert("Thanks, " + userName + "!");
```

Using the plus operator, the code combines—*concatenates*—three elements into the message: the string "Thanks, " plus the string represented by the variable **userName** plus the string "!"

Note that the first string includes a space. Without it, the alert would read, "Thanks,Susan!".

You can concatenate any combination of strings and variables, or all strings or all variables. For example, I can rewrite the last example this way.

```
1 var message = "Thanks, ";
2 var banger = "!";
3 alert(message + userName + banger);
```

Here it is, with three strings.

```
alert("Thanks, " + "Susan" + "!");
```

You can assign a concatenation to a variable.

```
1 var message = "Thanks, ";
2 var userName = "Susan";
3 var banger = "!";
4 var customMess = message + userName + banger;
5 alert(customMess);
```

If you put numbers in quotes, JavaScript concatenates them as strings rather than adding them. This code...

```
alert("2" + "2");
```

...displays the message "22".

If you mix strings and numbers...

```
alert("2 plus 2 equals " + 2 + 2);
```

...JavaScript automatically converts the numbers to strings, and displays the message "2 plus 2 equals 22".

Find the interactive coding exercises for this chapter at http://www.ASmarterWayToLearn.com/js/8.html

9
Prompts

A *prompt box* asks the user for some information and provides a response field for her answer.

This code asks the user the question "Your species?" and provides a default answer in the response field, "human". She can change the response. Whether she leaves the default response as-is or changes it to something else, her response is assigned to the variable.

```
var spec = prompt("Your species?", "human");
```

Prompt code is like alert code, with two differences.

In a prompt, you need a way to capture the user's response. That means you need to start by declaring a variable, followed by an equal sign.

In a prompt, you can specify a second string. This is the default response that appears in the field when the prompt displays. If the user leaves the default response as-is and just clicks **OK**, the default response is assigned to the variable. It's up to you whether you include a default response.

As you might expect, you can assign the strings to variables, then specify the variables instead of strings inside the parentheses.

```
1 var question = "Your species?";
2 var defaultAnswer = "human";
3 var spec = prompt(question, defaultAnswer);
```

The user's response is a text string. Even if the response is a number, it comes back as a string. For example, consider this code.

```
1 var numberOfCats = prompt("How many cats?");
2 var tooManyCats = numberOfCats + 1;
```

Since you're asking for a number, and the user is presumably entering one, you might expect the math in the second statement to work. For example, if the user enters 3, the variable **tooManyCats** should have a value of 4, you might think. But this is not the result we'll get. All responses to prompts come back as strings. When the string, "3", is linked with a plus to the number, 1, JavaScript converts the 1 to a string and concatenates. So the value of **tooManyCats** winds up being not 4 but "31". You'll learn how to solve this problem in a subsequent chapter.

If the user enters nothing and clicks OK, the variable is assigned an empty string: ""

If the user clicks **Cancel**, the variable is assigned a special value, null.

Coding Alternatives to Be Aware Of

- Some coders write **window.prompt** instead of, simply, **prompt**. This is a highly formal but perfectly correct way to write it. Most coders prefer the short form. We'll stick to the short form in this training.

- In the example above, some coders would use single rather than double quotation marks. This is legal, as long as it's a matching pair. But in a case like this, I'll ask you to use double quotation marks.

Find the interactive coding exercises for this chapter at http://www.ASmarterWayToLearn.com/js/9.html

10
if statements

Suppose you code a prompt that asks, "What does a dog wag?"

If the user answers correctly, you display an alert congratulating him. This is the code.

```
1 var x = prompt("What does a dog wag?");
2 if (x === "tail") {
3   alert("Correct!");
4 }
```

If the user enters "tail" in the prompt field, the congratulations alert displays. If he enters something else, nothing happens. (This simplified code doesn't allow for other correct answers, like "his tail." I don't want to get into that now.)

There's a lot to take in here. Let's break it down.

An if statement always begins with **if**. The space that separates it from the parenthesis is new to you. I've taught you to code alerts and prompts with the opening parenthesis running up against the keyword: **alert("Hi");** Now I'm asking you *not* to do that in an *if* statement. It's purely a matter of style, but common style rules sanction this inconsistency.

Following the **if** keyword-plus-space is the condition that's being tested—does the variable that's been assigned the user's response have a value of "tail"?

The condition is enclosed in parentheses.

If the condition tests true, something happens. Any number of statements might execute. In this case, only one statement executes: a congratulatory alert displays.

Following my style rules, the statement or statements that execute if the condition tests true are indented 2 spaces.

The first line of an *if* statement ends with an opening curly bracket. An entire *if* statement ends with a closing curly bracket on its own line. Note that this is an exception to the rule that a statement ends with a semicolon. It's common to omit the semicolon when it's a complex statement that's paragraph-like and ends in a curly bracket.

But what about that triple equal sign? You might think that it should just be an equal sign, but the equal sign is reserved for *assigning* a value to a variable. If you're *testing* a variable for a value, you can't use the single equal sign.

If you forget this rule and use a single equal sign when you should use the triple equal sign, the code won't run properly.

As you might expect, you can use a variable instead of a string in the example code.

```
1 var correctAnswer = "tail";
2 if (x === correctAnswer) {
3    alert("Correct!");
4 }
```

When a condition is met, you can have any number of statements execute.

```
1 var correctAnswer = "tail";
2 if (x === correctAnswer) {
3    score++;
4    userIQ = "genius";
5    alert("Correct!");
6 }
```

Coding Alternatives to Be Aware Of

- Some coders write simple if statements without curly brackets, which is legal. Some put the opening curly bracket on its own line. Some put the whole if statement, if it's simple, on a single line. I find it easiest not to have to make case-by-case decisions, so I format all if statements the same way, as shown in the example. In the exercises, I'll ask you to follow these style rules for all *if* statements.

- In most cases, a double equal sign == is just as good as a triple equal sign ===. However, there is a slight technical difference, which you may never need to know. Again, to keep things simple, I always use the triple equal sign.

Find the interactive coding exercises for this chapter at:
http://www.ASmarterWayToLearn.com/js/10.html

11
Comparison operators

Let's talk a little more about ===. It's a type of *comparison operator*, specifically an *equality operator*. As you learned in the last chapter, you use it to compare two things to see if they're equal.

You can use the equality operator to compare a variable with a string, a variable with a number, a variable with a math expression, or a variable with a variable. And you can use it to compare various combinations. All of the following are legal first lines in *if* statements:

```
if (fullName === "Mark" + " " + "Myers") {
if (fullName === firstName + " " + "Myers") {
if (fullName === firstName + " " + lastName) {
if (totalCost === 81.50 + 135) {
if (totalCost === materialsCost + 135) {
if (totalCost === materialsCost + laborCost) {
if (x + y === a - b) {
```

When you're comparing strings, the equality operator is case-sensitive. "Rose" does not equal "rose."

Another comparison operator, !==, is the opposite of ===. It means is not equal to.

```
1 if (yourTicketNumber !== 487208) {
2    alert("Better luck next time.");
3 }
```

Like ===, the not-equal operator can be used to compare numbers, strings, variables, math expressions, and combinations.

Like ===, string comparisons using the not-equal operator are case-sensitive. It's true that "Rose" !== "rose".

Here are 4 more comparison operators, usually used to compare numbers.

> is greater than

< is less than

>= is greater than or equal to

<= is less than or equal to

In the examples below, all the conditions are true.

```
if (1 > 0) {
if (0 < 1) {
if (1 >= 0) {
if (1 >= 1) {
if (0 <= 1) {
if (1 <= 1) {
```

Coding Alternatives to Be Aware Of

Just as the double equal sign can usually be used instead of the triple equal sign, **!=** can usually be used instead of **!==**. In the exercises, I'll ask you to stick to **!==**.

Find the interactive coding exercises for this chapter at http://www.ASmarterWayToLearn.com/js/11.html

12
if...else and *else if* statements

The *if* statements you've coded so far have been all-or-nothing. If the condition tested true, something happened. If the condition tested false, nothing happened.

```
1 var x = prompt("What does a dog wag?");
2 if (x === "tail") {
3   alert("Correct!");
4 }
```

Quite often, you want something to happen either way. For example:

```
1 var x = prompt("What does a dog wag?");
2 if (x === "tail") {
3   alert("Correct!");
4 }
5 if (x !== "tail") {
6   alert("Wrong answer");
7 }
```

In this example, we have two *if* statements, one testing for "tail," and another testing for not-"tail". So all cases are covered, with one alert or another displaying, depending on what the user has entered.

The code works, but it's more verbose than necessary. The following code is more concise and, as a bonus, more readable.

```
1 if (x === "tail") {
2   alert("Correct!");
3 }
4 else {
5   alert("Wrong answer");
6 }
```

In the style convention I follow, the **else** part has exactly the same formatting as the **if** part.

As in the **if** part, any number of statements can execute within the **else** part.

```
1 var correctAnswer = "tail";
2 if (x === correctAnswer) {
3   alert("Correct!");
4 }
5 else {
6   score--;
7   askAgain = "yes";
8   alert("Incorrect");
9 }
```

else if is used if all tests above have failed and you want to test another condition.

```
1  var correctAnswer = "tail";
2  if (x === correctAnswer) {
3    alert("Correct!");
4  }
5  else if (x === "tale") {
6    alert("Incorrect but close");
7  }
8  else {
9    alert("Incorrect");
10 }
```

In a series of if tests, JavaScript stops testing whenever a condition tests true.

Coding Alternatives to Be Aware Of

There are so many ways to format if statements and their variations that the range of possibilities is almost endless. I'm partial to the format I've showed you, because it's easy to learn and produces readable code. I'll ask you to stick to this format throughout the exercises.

Find the interactive coding exercises for this chapter at http://www.ASmarterWayToLearn.com/js/12.html

13
Testing sets of conditions

Using the *if* statement, you've learned to test for a condition. If the condition is met, one or more statements execute. But suppose not one but two conditions have to be met in order for a test to succeed.

For example, if a guy weighs more than 300 pounds, he's just a great big guy. But if he weighs more than 300 pounds and runs 40 yards in under 6 seconds? You're going to invite him to try out for the NFL as a lineman. You can test for a combination of conditions in JavaScript by using...

&& —which is the equivalent of *and* in English. Here's the code.

```
1 if (weight > 300 && time < 6) {
2    alert("Come to our tryout!");
3 }
4 else {
5    alert("Come to our cookout!");
6 }
```

You can chain any number of conditions together.

```
1 if (weight > 300 && time < 6 && age > 17 && gender ===
"male") {
2    alert("Come to our tryout!");
3 }
4 else {
5    alert("Come to our cookout!");
6 }
```

You can also test for any of a set of conditions The operator is || — which is the equivalent of *or* in English. Here's an example.

```
1 if (SAT > avg || GPA > 2.5 || sport === "football") {
2   alert("Welcome to Bubba State!");
3 }
4 else {
5   alert("Have you looked into appliance repair?");
6 }
```

If in line 1 any or all of the conditions are true, the first alert displays. If none of them are true (line 4), the second alert displays.

You can combine any number of **and** and **or** conditions. When you do, you create ambiguities. Take this line...

```
if (age > 65 || age < 21 && res === "U.S.") {
```

This can be read in either of two ways.

The first way it can be read: If the person is over 65 or under 21 and, in addition to either of these conditions, is also a resident of the U.S. Under this interpretation, both columns need to be true in the following table in order for the overall *if* statement to be true...

Over 65 or under 21	Resident of U.S.

The second way it can be read: If the person is over 65 and living anywhere or is under 21 and a resident of the U.S. Under this interpretation, if either column in the following table is true, the overall *if* statement is true.

Over 65	Under 21 and U.S. resident

It's the same problem you face when you combine mathematical expressions. And you solve it the same way: with parentheses.

In the following code, if the subject is over 65 and a U.S. resident, it's a pass. Or, if the subject is under 21 and a U.S. resident, the overall *if* statement is true.

```
if ((age > 65 || age < 21) && res === "U.S.") {
```

In the following code, if the subject is over 65 and living anywhere, it's a pass. Or, if the subject is under 21 and living in the U.S., the overall *if* statement is true.

```
if (age > 65 || (age < 21 && res === "U.S.")) {
```

Find the interactive coding exercises for this chapter at
http://www.ASmarterWayToLearn.com/js/13.html

14
if statements nested

Check out this code.

```
1 if ((x === y || a === b) && c === d) {
2   g = h;
3 }
4 else {
5    e = f;
6 }
```

In the code above, if either of the first conditions is true, and, in addition, the third condition is true, then **g** is assigned **h**. Otherwise, **e** is assigned **f**.

There's another way to code this, using nesting.

```
1   if (c === d) {
2      if (x === y) {
3          g = h;
4      }
5      else if (a === b) {
6          g = h;
7      }
8      else {
9          e = f;
10     }
11 }
12 else {
13    e = f;
14 }
```

Nest levels are communicated to JavaScript by the positions of the curly brackets. There are three blocks nested inside the top-level **if**. If the condition tested by the top-level **if**—that **c** has the same value as **d**—is false, none of the blocks nested inside executes. The opening curly bracket on line 1 and the closing curly bracket on line 11 enclose all the nested code, telling JavaScript that everything inside is second-level.

For readability, a lower level is indented 2 spaces beyond the level above it.

In the relatively simple set of tests and outcomes shown in this example, I would prefer to use the more concise structure of multiple conditions. But when things get really complicated, nested ifs are a good way to go.

Find the interactive coding exercises for this chapter at http://www.ASmarterWayToLearn.com/js/14.html

15
Arrays

Let's assign some string values to some variables.

```
var city0 = "Atlanta";
var city1 = "Baltimore";
var city2 = "Chicago";
var city3 = "Denver";
var city4 = "Los Angeles";
var city5 = "Seattle";
```

The variable names are all the same, except they end in different numbers. I could have named the variables **buffy**, **the**, **vampireSlayer**, and so on if I'd wanted to, but I chose to name them this way because of where this discussion is going.

Now, having made these assignments, if I code...

```
alert("Welcome to " + city3);
```

...an alert displays saying, "Welcome to Denver". I'm going to show you another type of variable, one that will come in handy for many tasks that you'll learn about in later chapters. I'm talking about a type of variable called an *array*. Whereas an ordinary variable has a single value assigned to it—for example, 9 or "Paris"—an array is a variable that can have multiple values assigned to it. You define an array this way:

```
var cities = ["Atlanta", "Baltimore", "Chicago", "Denver",
"Los Angeles", "Seattle"];
```

In the example at the beginning of this chapter, I ended each variable name with a number. **city0** was "Atlanta", **city1** was "Baltimore", and so on. The array I just defined is similar, but in the case of an array defined the way I just defined one, JavaScript numbers the different values, or elements, automatically. (You can control the numbering yourself by defining elements individually. See below.) And you refer to each element by writing the array name—cities in this case—followed by a number enclosed in square brackets. **cities[0]** is "Atlanta", **cities[1]** is "Baltimore", and so on.

Because JavaScript automatically numbers array elements, you have no say in the numbering. The first element in the list always has an *index* of 0, the second element an index of 1, and so on.

This is the alert I coded above, but now specifying an array element instead of an ordinary variable.

```
alert("Welcome to " + cities[3]);
```

An array can be assigned any type of value that you can assign to ordinary variables. You can even mix the different types in the same array (not that you would ordinarily want to).

```
var mixedArray = [1, "Bob", "Now is", true];
```

In the example above, **mixedArray[0]** has a numerical value of 1, **mixedArray[1]** has a string value of "Bob", and so on.

Things to keep in mind:

- The first item always has an index of 0, not 1. This means that if the last item in the list has an index of 9, there are 10 items in the list.

- The same naming rules you learned for ordinary variables apply. Only letters, numbers, $ and _ are legal. The first character can't be a number. No spaces.

- Coders often prefer to make array names plural—cities instead of city, for example—since an array is a list of things.

- Like an ordinary variable, you declare an array only once. If you assign new values to an array that has already been declared, you drop the var.

Find the interactive coding exercises for this chapter at http://www.ASmarterWayToLearn.com/js/15.html

16
Arrays: Adding and removing elements

As you learned in earlier chapters, you can declare an empty variable, one that doesn't have a value. Then you can assign it a value whenever you like. And you can change its value at will. You can do all these things with an array, as well.

This is how you declare an empty array.

```
var pets = [];
```

Assume that the array **pets** has already been declared. This is how you assign values to it.

```
1 pets[0] = "dog";
2 pets[1] = "cat";
3 pets[2] = "bird";
```

In the example above, I defined the first three elements of the array, in order. But you can legally leave gaps in an array if you choose to (not that you normally would). For example, suppose you start with the same empty array and code these lines.

```
1 pets[3] = "lizard";
2 pets[6] = "snake";
```

Now, if you refer to **pets[3]**, you'll get "lizard". If you refer to **pets[6]**, you'll get "snake". But if you refer to pets[0] through **pets[2]** or **pets[4]** or **pets[5]**, you'll get **undefined**.

You can assign additional values to an array that already has values. Assume that the first three elements of the array pets are "dog", "cat", and "bird". Then you write this code.

```
1 pets[3] = "lizard";
2 pets[4] = "fish";
3 pets[5] = "gerbil";
4 pets[6] = "snake";
```

Now the array has 7 elements: "dog", "cat", "bird", "lizard", "fish", "gerbil", and "snake".

If you assign a new value to an array element that already has one, the old value is replaced by the new one.

Using the keyword, **pop**, you can remove the last element of an array.

Suppose you have an array, **pets**, whose elements are "dog", "cat", and "bird". The following code deletes the last element, "bird", leaving a two-element array.

```
pets.pop();
```

You can assign the deleted last element to a variable.

```
var lastElement = pets.pop();
```

Now the variable **lastElement** represents the string "bird."

Using the keyword, **push**, you can add one or more elements to the end of an array.

Suppose you have that same array consisting of "dog", "cat", and "bird". The following code adds two new elements to the end of the array.

```
pets.push("fish", "ferret");
```

Find the interactive coding exercises for this chapter at http://www.ASmarterWayToLearn.com/js/16.html

17
Arrays: Removing and inserting elements

Use the **shift** method to remove an element from the beginning of an array.

Suppose you have an array, **pets**, whose elements are "dog", "cat", and "bird". The following removes the first element, "dog", leaving you with a two-element array.

```
pets.shift();
```

To add one or more elements to the beginning of an array, use the **unshift** method. The following code adds two elements to the beginning of the array.

```
pets.unshift("fish", "ferret");
```

Use the **splice** method to insert one or more elements anywhere in an array, while optionally removing one or more elements that come after it. Suppose you have an array with the elements "dog", "cat", "fly", "bug", "ox". The following code adds "pig", "duck", and "emu" after "cat" while removing "fly" and "bug".

```
pets.splice(2, 2, "pig", "duck", "emu");
```

The first digit inside the parentheses is the index of the position where you want to start adding if you're adding and deleting if you're deleting. The second digit is the number of existing elements to remove, starting with the first element that comes after the element(s) that you're splicing in. The code above leaves you with an array consisting of "dog", "cat", "pig", "duck", "emu", and "ox".

You could make additions without removing any elements. The following code adds "pig", "duck", and "emu" without removing any elements.

```
pets.splice(2, 0, "pig", "duck", "emu");
```

You can also remove elements without adding any. If you start with the elements "dog", "cat", "fly", "bug", and "ox", the following code removes two elements starting at index 2—"fly" and "bug". This leaves "dog", "cat", and "ox".

```
pets.splice(2, 2);
```

Use the **slice** method to copy one or more consecutive elements in any position and put them into a new array. If you start with an array, **pets**, consisting of "dog", "cat", "fly", "bug", and "ox", the following code copies "fly" and "bug" to the new array **noPets** and leaves the original array, **pets**, unchanged.

```
var noPets = pets.slice(2, 4);
```

The first digit inside the parentheses is the index of the first element to be copied. The second digit is the index of the element after the last element to be copied.

Two things could trip you up here:

Since the first index number inside the parentheses specifies the first element to be copied, you might think the second index number specifies the last element to be copied. In fact, the second number specifies the index number of the element *after* the last element to be copied.

You must assign the sliced elements to an array. It could, of course, be the same array from which you're doing the slicing. In that case, you'd be reducing the original array to only the copied elements.

Find the interactive coding exercises for this chapter at http://www.ASmarterWayToLearn.com/js/17.html

18
for loops

You know the song "99 Bottles of Beer on the Wall"? If you're teaching someone the song, you could give them these instructions:

1. Sing "99 bottles of beer on the wall, 99 bottles of beer."

2. Sing "Take one down and pass it around, 98 bottles of beer on the wall."

3. Sing "98 bottles of beer on the wall, 98 bottles of beer."

4. Sing "Take one down and pass it around, 97 bottles of beer on the wall."

5. Sing "97 bottles of beer on the wall, 97 bottles of beer."

6. Sing "Take one down and pass it around, 96 bottles of beer on the wall."

...and so on, for 192 more lines of instructions.

But that isn't how you'd give the instructions, is it? You'd be more concise. You'd say something like this:

Sing "99 bottles of beer on the wall, 99 bottles of beer. Take one down and pass it around, 98 bottles of beer on the wall." Repeat this, subtracting 1 each time, until there are no more bottles of beer on the wall.

In coding, you run into the bottles-of-beer situation quite often. For example, suppose you've offered to check if the user's city is one of the 5 cleanest in the U.S. The user has entered her city, and you've assigned her city to the variable **cityToCheck**.

You've already assigned the list of the 5 cleanest cities to the array **cleanestCities**.

```
var cleanestCities = ["Cheyenne", "Santa Fe", "Tucson",
"Great Falls", "Honolulu"];
```

Now you go through the array to see if there's a match with the user's city. If there is, you display an alert telling the user her city is one of the cleanest. If there's no match, you display an alert telling the user her city isn't on the list.

```
1   if (cityToCheck === cleanestCities[0]) {
2      alert("It's one of the cleanest cities");
3   }
4   else if (cityToCheck === cleanestCities[1]) {
5      alert("It's one of the cleanest cities");
6   }
7   else if (cityToCheck === cleanestCities[2]) {
8      alert("It's one of the cleanest cities");
9   }
10  else if (cityToCheck === cleanestCities[3]) {
11     alert("It's one of the cleanest cities");
12  }
13  else if (cityToCheck === cleanestCities[4]) {
14     alert("It's one of the cleanest cities");
15  }
16  else {
17     alert("It's not on the list");
18  }
```

Conveniently, JavaScript provides a more concise coding approach. Here's a *for* loop that accomplishes most of what the verbose code in the example above accomplishes.

```
1   for (var i = 0; i <= 4; i++) {
2      if (cityToCheck === cleanestCities[i]) {
3         alert("It's one of the cleanest cities");
4      }
5   }
```

Let me break down the first line for you.

The first line begins with the keyword **for**.

The three specifications that define the loop are inside the parentheses.

1. A variable that counts iterations and also serves as the changing array index is declared and set to a starting value, in this case 0.

2. The limit on the loop is defined. In this case, the loop is to keep running as long as the counter doesn't exceed 4. Since the counter, in this case, is starting at 0, the loop will run 5 times.

3. What happens to the counter at the end of every loop. In this case, the counter is incremented each time.

The three specifications inside the parentheses are always in the same order:

1. What to call the counter (usually **i**) and what number to start it at (typically 0)

2. How many loops to run (in this case, the number of elements in the array)

3. How to change the counter after each iteration (typically to add 1 each time through)

Things to keep in mind:

- In the example, the counter, **i**, serves two purposes. It keeps track of the number of iterations so looping can halt at the right point. And it serves as the index number of the array, allowing the code to progress through all the elements of the array as the counter increments with each iteration.

- There is nothing sacred about using **i** as the counter. You can use any legal variable name. But coders usually use **i** because it keeps the first line compact, and because traditionally **i** stands for "integer." I think of it as standing for "iteration."

- In the example, the initial count is 0, the index number of the first element of the array. But it could be any number, depending on your needs.

- In the example, the counter increments with each iteration. But, depending on your needs, you can decrement it, increase it by 2 or another number, or change it in some other way each time through.

- In the example, I specify that the loop is to run as long as **i <= 4**. Alternatively, I could have specified **i < 5**. Either way, since the counter starts at 0, the loop runs 5 times.

Find the interactive coding exercises for this chapter at:
http://www.ASmarterWayToLearn.com/js/18.html

19
for loops:
Flags, Booleans, array length,
and loopus interruptus

There are several problems with the *for* loop example I gave you in the last chapter. The first problem is a potential communication problem. If a match between the user's city and the list of cleanest cities is found, a confirming alert displays. But if there is no match, nothing happens. The user is left in the dark. If no match is found, we need to display an alert saying so. But how do we do that?

We do it with a *flag*. A flag is just a variable that starts out with a default value that you give it, and then is switched to a different value under certain conditions. In our example, let's say we define **matchFound** as the flag.

```
var matchFound = "no";
```

If a match is found, the value of the flag is changed. At the end, if the flag hasn't been changed—if it still has the original value of "no"—it means no match was found, and so we display an alert saying the city isn't on the list.

```
1   var matchFound = "no";
2   for (var i = 0; i <= 4; i++) {
3     if (cityToCheck === cleanestCities[i]) {
4       matchFound = "yes";
5       alert("It's one of the cleanest cities");
6     }
7   }
8   if (matchFound === "no") {
9     alert("It's not on the list");
10  }
```

This works, but rather than assigning the strings "no" and "yes" to the switch, it's conventional to use the *Boolean* values **false** and **true**.

```
1   var matchFound = false;
2   for (var i = 0; i <= 4; i++) {
3     if (cityToCheck === cleanestCities[i]) {
4       matchFound = true;
5       alert("It's one of the cleanest cities");
6     }
7   }
8   if (matchFound === false) {
9     alert("It's not on the list");
10  }
```

There are only two Booleans, **true** and **false**. Note that they aren't enclosed in quotes.

The next problem with our example is that it potentially wastes computing cycles. Suppose on the second loop a match is found and the alert displays. The way the loop is coded, the loop goes on looping all the way to the end. This is unnecessary, since we got our answer in the second loop. The problem is solved with the keyword **break**.

```
1   var matchFound = false;
2   for (var i = 0; i <= 4; i++) {
3     if (cityToCheck === cleanestCities[i]) {
4       matchFound = true;
5       alert("It's one of the cleanest cities");
6       break;
7     }
8   }
9   if (matchFound === false) {
10    alert("It's not on the list");
11  }
```

The last problem: In the example, I assume that the number of elements in the array is known. But what if it isn't? JavaScript has a way of finding out. The following code assigns the number of elements in the array **cleanestCities** to the variable **numElements**.

`var numElements = cleanestCities.length;`

Now we can limit the number of loops to the count that JavaScript comes up with.

```
1  var numElements = cleanestCities.length;
2  var matchFound = false;
3  for (var i = 0; i < numElements; i++) {
4    if (cityToCheck === cleanestCities[i]) {
5    matchFound = true;
6    alert("It's one of the cleanest cities");
7    break;
8    }
9  }
10 if (matchFound === false) {
11   alert("It's not on the list");
12 }
```

Now the loop keeps going as long as **i** is less than the number of elements. (Since the length number is 1-based and the **i** number is 0-based, we need to stop 1 short of the length.)

Find the interactive coding exercises for this chapter at: http://www.ASmarterWayToLearn.com/js/19.html

20
for loops nested

Atlantic Records has hired you and me to generate a list of names for future rap stars. To make things easy, we'll start by making separate lists of some first names and last names.

First Names	Last Names
BlueRay	Zzz
Upchuck	Burp
Lojack	Dogbone
Gizmo	Droop
Do-Rag	

By combining each of the first names with each of the last names, we can generate 20 different full names for rappers.

Starting with "BlueRay," we go through the list of last names, generating...

BlueRay Zzz
BlueRay Burp
BlueRay Dogbone
BlueRay Droop

We move to the next first name, "Upchuck." Again, we go through the list of last names, generating...

Upchuck Zzz
Upchuck Burp
Upchuck Dogbone
Upchuck Droop

And so on, combining each first name with each last name.

But look, why not have JavaScript do the repetitive work? We'll use nested *for* statements.

```
1   var firstNames = ["BlueRay ", "Upchuck ", "Lojack ",
"Gizmo ", "Do-Rag "];
2   var lastNames = ["Zzz", "Burp", "Dogbone", "Droop"];
3   var fullNames = [];
5   for (var i = 0; i < firstNames.length; i++) {
6     for (var j = 0; j < lastNames.length; j++) {
7       fullNames.push(firstNames[i] + lastNames[j]);
9     }
10  }
```

Things to think about:

- The inner loop runs a complete cycle of iterations on each iteration of the outer loop. If the outer loop counter is **i** and the inner loop counter is **j**, **j** will loop through 0, 1, 2, and all the way to the end while **i** is on 0. Then **i** will increment to 1, and **j** will loop through all of its values again. The outer loop is the minute hand of a clock. The inner loop is the second hand.

- You can have as many levels of nesting as you like.

- A nested loop is indented 2 spaces beyond its outer loop.

Find the interactive coding exercises for this chapter at http://www.ASmarterWayToLearn.com/js/20.html

21
Changing case

You ask the user to enter her city. Then you check her city against a list of the 5 cleanest cities.

If the user enters "Cheyenne" or any of the other cleanest cities, your code displays an alert telling her that it's one of the cleanest cities.

But what if she enters "cheyenne" instead of "Cheyenne"—as some users inevitably will? When that happens, there will be no match. JavaScript is literal-minded.

A human knows that in this context "cheyenne" means "Cheyenne." But JavaScript doesn't. We need some way to get JavaScript to recognize the uncapitalized version as a match.

One way would be to expand the **cleanestCities** array to include the uncapitalized versions of all the city names:

```
var cleanestCities = ["Cheyenne", "cheyenne", "Santa Fe",
"santa fe", "Tucson", "tucson", "Great Falls", "great
falls", "Honolulu", "honolulu"];
```

This works up to a point, but it's a lot of extra coding. Plus, if the user enters "santa Fe," "Santa fe," or "sAnta Fe," we're back to the original problem. To cover all these possibilities and others, it would take a mile of code.

The solution is to code the array elements in lower-case, and convert the user's input, whatever it is, to lower-case, so we always have apples to compare with apples.

```
1 var cityToCheck = prompt("Enter your city");
2 cityToCheck = cityToCheck.toLowerCase();
3 var cleanestCities = ["cheyenne", "santa fe", "tucson",
"great falls", "honolulu"];
4 for (var i = 0; i <= 4; i++) {
5   if (cityToCheck === cleanestCities[i]) {
6     alert("It's one of the cleanest cities");
7   }
8 }
```

Line 2 is what's new here:

```
2 cityToCheck = cityToCheck.toLowerCase();
```

The converted string is assigned to a variable. In this case, it's the same variable whose string is being converted, **cityToCheck**. Note that the keyword **toLowerCase** must be in camelCase.

Note too that the **toLowerCase** method converts all the characters of the string to lower-case, not just the initial letters. For example, "ChEyEnNe" becomes "cheyenne."

You could go the other way and convert everything to upper-case, then test against "CHEYENNE," "SANTA FE, " etc. Most coders prefer the lower-case method. To convert the string to upper-case, you'd write:

```
2 cityToCheck = cityToCheck.toUpperCase();
```

Find the interactive coding exercises for this chapter at http://www.ASmarterWayToLearn.com/js/21.html

22
Strings: Measuring length and extracting parts

You've asked the user to give you the name of a city. You want to convert the name she's given you to a name with an initial cap. Whether she's input "boston," "BOSTON," or "bosTon," you want to normalize the input to "Boston." The **toLowerCase** and **toUpperCase** methods you learned in the last chapter won't get the job done on their own, because they make the same wholesale change to every character in the string. But if you break the string up into two segments, you can use these methods to get the string into the shape you want. (For now, I'll ignore the possibility that the city name might be made up of two or more words, like New Orleans or Sault Ste. Marie.)

To copy a section of a string, you use the **slice** method. Suppose the user has entered a string, and the string has been assigned to the variable **cityToCheck**. The following code copies the first character of the string and assigns it to the variable **firstChar**. The original value of **cityToCheck** doesn't change. If **cityToCheck** is "Boston", **firstChar** is "B".

```
var firstChar = cityToCheck.slice(0, 1);
```

Things to be aware of:

- A string is indexed like an array. Only, instead of each index number referring to an element, it refers to a character.

- Like array indexing, string indexing begins with 0.

- In the **slice** method, the first number inside the parentheses is the index of the first character in the slice. The second number is not, however, the last character in the slice. It's the first character *after* the slice. If you subtract the first index from the second index, you'll always get the length of the slice.

Here's another example.

```
var someChars = cityToCheck.slice(2, 5);
```

Again let's say that the string is "Boston". The slice begins with the index-2 (the third) character, "s". It ends with the character before the index-5 character, "n". **someChars** is "sto".

If you omit the second number inside the parentheses, JavaScript includes all the characters to the end of the string.

```
var someChars = cityToCheck.slice(2);
```

The slice begins with the index-2 (the third) character, "s". Since no cutoff at the end is specified, the slice ends with the last character of the string. **someChars** is "ston".

Now we have a way to capitalize the first character of a string and insure that the remaining letters are lower-case.

```
1 var firstChar = cityToCheck.slice(0, 1);
2 var otherChars = cityToCheck.slice(1);
3 firstChar = firstChar.toUpperCase();
4 otherChars = otherChars.toLowerCase();
5 var cappedCity = firstChar + otherChars;
```

Here's what happens in the code above, line-by-line:

1. Copies the first character of the string and assigns it to the variable **firstChar**.

2. Copies all the characters from the second one to the end and assigns them to the variable **otherChars**.

3. Caps the first character.

4. Lower-cases the other characters.

5. Concatenates both parts to re-form the whole string.

Sometimes it's useful to know how many characters are in a string. For example, suppose you want to slice the first three characters from any string that exceeds three characters in length, slicing "Nov" from "November". To find the number of characters in a string, you use the same language you've already learned to find the number of elements in an array.

```
1 var month = prompt("Enter a month");
2 var charsInMonth = month.length;
3 if (charsInMonth > 3) {
4   monthAbbrev = month.slice(0, 3);
5 }
```

Line 2 counts the characters in the string and assigns the number to the variable **charsInMonth**.

Being able to measure the number of characters in a string can come in handy. For example, suppose you want to loop through a string, checking to see if it has any double spaces in it. You can use the character count as the loop limiter. Here's some code that checks for double spaces in a string and displays an alert if they're found.

```
1 var str = prompt("Enter some text");
2 var numChars = str.length;
3 for (var i = 0; i < numChars; i++) {
4   if (str.slice(i, i + 2) === "  ") {
5     alert("No double spaces allowed!");
6     break;
7   }
8 }
```

Line 2 counts the number of characters in the string and assigns the number to the variable **numChars**. In line 3, this number is used as the loop limiter. The loop continues to run only as long as the counter, **i**, is less than the number of characters in the string. (Remember, the length is 1-based, and the counter is 0-based, so the loop has to stop 1 short of the length number.) Line 4 moves through the string character-by-character, examining each 2-character segment, looking for double spaces.

Find the interactive coding exercises for this chapter at http://www.ASmarterWayToLearn.com/js/22.html

23
Strings: Finding segments

The New Yorker magazine doesn't allow the phrase "World War II. " They say it should be "the Second World War." So let's search the following sentence for the banned characters and replace them with the phrase that the New Yorker prefers.

> It is startling to think that, even in the darkest depths of World War II, J. R. R. Tolkien was writing the trilogy, which contains, with the weird applicability available only to poetry and myth, the essential notion that the good gray wizard can understand the evil magi precisely because he is just enough like them to grasp their minds and motives in ways that they cannot grasp his.

You already know a way to find the banned segment and replace it. Suppose the paragraph above has been assigned to the variable **text**.

```
1 for (var i = 0; i < text.length; i++) {
2    if (text.slice(i, i + 12) === "World War II") {
3      text = text.slice(0, i) + "the Second World War" +
text.slice(i + 12);
4    }
5 }
```

The code loops through the string looking for "World War II." Line 2 progresses through the string character-by-character, examining each 12-character sequence. On each iteration, if it finds "World War II," line 3 concatenates three segments: all the characters preceding "World War II," the substitute phrase "the Second World War," and then all the characters following "World War II."

But JavaScript has a more efficient way to accomplish this, using the **indexOf** method.

```
var firstChar = text.indexOf("World War II");
```

If the segment exists, the method finds the index of the first character of the segment and assigns it to the variable **firstChar**. If the segment doesn't exist, the method assigns -1 to the variable, so you know it's not there.

Now we can replace the banned phrase with the preferred phrase with less coding.

```
1 var firstChar = text.indexOf("World War II");
2 if (firstChar !== -1) {
3   text = text.slice(0, firstChar) + "the Second World
War" + text.slice(firstChar + 12);
4 }
```

Line 1 checks for the phrase, assigning the index of the first character of the phrase to the variable **firstChar**—if the phrase is found. If it isn't found, -1 is assigned to the variable. If the variable doesn't have the value -1 (line 2)—if the phrase has been found—the concatenation in line 3 combines the text that precedes "World War II" with the new phrase.

The **indexOf** method finds only the first instance of the segment you're looking for. In the example above, you could overcome this limitation by looping. You'd change the first instance of "World War II" to "the Second World War," then in the next loop iteration, find the next surviving instance and change that, and so on.

To find the last instance of a segment in a string, use **lastIndexOf**. The following code finds the index of the first character of the last instance of the segment, the second "be". The variable **segIndex** winds up with a value of 16, the index of "b" in the second "be".

```
1 var text = "To be or not to be.";
2 var segIndex = text.lastIndexOf("be");
```

Find the interactive coding exercises for this chapter at http://www.ASmarterWayToLearn.com/js/23.html

24
Strings: Finding a character at a location

The user has entered his first name. The string has been assigned to the variable **firstName**. You want to extract the first character. You already know one way to do it.

```
var firstChar = firstName.slice(0, 1);
```

Here's an alternate way to do it that's more direct.

```
var firstChar = firstName.charAt(0);
```

The code above finds a single character at index-0 (the beginning) of the string represented by the variable **firstName** and assigns it to the variable **firstChar**.

The following code finds the last character in the string.

```
var lastChar = name.charAt(name.length - 1);
```

The following code cycles through a string looking for an exclamation point. If the character is found, an alert displays.

```
1 for (var i = 0; i < text.length; i++) {
2   if (text.charAt(i) === "!") {
3     alert("Exclamation point found!");
4     break;
5   }
6 }
```

Note: The **charAt** method can only identify the character at a particular location. It can't change the character at a location.

Find the interactive coding exercises for this chapter at http://www.ASmarterWayToLearn.com/js/24.html

25
Strings: Replacing characters

In previous chapters you learned two different ways to replace "World War II" with "the Second World War" in a string. First, there was the loop-and-slice approach.

```
1 for (var i = 0; i < text.length; i++) {
2   if (text.slice(i, i + 12) === "World War II") {
3     text = text.slice(0, i) + "the Second World War" +
text.slice(i + 12);
4   }
5 }
```

You improved on that rather crude approach when you learned the **indexOf** method.

```
1 var firstChar = text.indexOf("World War II");
2 if (firstChar !== -1) {
3   text = text.slice(0, firstChar) + "the Second World
War" + text.slice(firstChar + 12);
4 }
```

But JavaScript provides a more straightforward way still, the **replace** method.

```
var newText = text.replace("World War II", "the Second
World War");
```

The first string inside the parentheses is the segment to be replaced. The second string is the segment to be inserted. In the above code, the segment "World War II" is replaced by the segment "the Second World War" in the string represented by the variable text, and the revised string is assigned to the new variable **newText**.

If you assign the revised string to a new variable, as in the example above, the original string is preserved. If you want the original string to be replaced by the revised string, assign the revised string to the original variable.

```
text = text.replace("World War II", "the Second World
War");
```

In the examples above, only the first instance of a string is replaced. If you want to replace all instances, you must let JavaScript know that you want a *global replace*.

```
var newText = text.replace(/World War II/g, "the Second
World War");
```

In a global replace, you enclose the segment to be replaced by slashes instead of quotation marks, and follow the closing slash with "g" for "global." The segment to be inserted is enclosed by quotation marks, as in a one-time replace.

Find the interactive coding exercises for this chapter at http://www.ASmarterWayToLearn.com/js/25.html

26
Rounding numbers

You run an online music service where customers rate each song. You aggregate all the customer ratings and average them, awarding a song from zero to five stars. Usually, averaging produces a fraction. You need to round it to the nearest integer so you can translate the number into stars. Suppose the average has been assigned to the variable **scoreAvg**. Here's the code that rounds it to the nearest integer.

```
var numberOfStars = Math.round(scoreAvg);
```

Things to keep in mind:

- **Math.** is how all math functions begin. The "M" must be capped.

- The function rounds up when the decimal is .5. It rounds 1.5 to 2, 2.5 to 3, etc. It rounds -1.5 to -1, -2.5 to -2, etc.

When the result is assigned to a new variable, as in the example above, the unrounded number enclosed in parentheses is preserved. But you can assign the rounded number to the original variable, and the unrounded number will be replaced by the rounded number.

```
scoreAvg = Math.round(scoreAvg);
```

Instead of a variable, you can enclose a literal number in the parentheses.

```
var scoreAvg = Math.round(.0678437);
```

To force JavaScript to round up to the nearest integer, no matter how small the fraction, use **ceil** instead of **round**. The following code rounds .000001, which would normally round down to 0, up to the nearest integer, 1.

```
var scoreAvg = Math.ceil(.000001);
```

ceil stands for "ceiling." It rounds .000001 up to 1, -.000001 up to

0, 1.00001 up to 2, and so on.

To force JavaScript to round down to the nearest integer, no matter how large the fraction, use **floor** instead of **round**. The following code rounds .999999, which would normally round up to 1, down to 0.

```
var scoreAvg = Math.floor(.999999);
```

floor rounds .999999 down to 0, 1.9 down to 1, -.000001 down to -1, and so on.

Find the interactive coding exercises for this chapter at http://www.ASmarterWayToLearn.com/js/26.html

27
Generating random numbers

Suppose you want to simulate the throw of a die. In the simulation, you want it to randomly come up 1, 2, 3, 4, 5, or 6. The first step is to ask JavaScript to generate a random number. (Well, it's almost random, technically known as *pseudo-random*, but it's close enough to random for most purposes.)

The following code generates a pseudo-random number, with 16 decimal places, ranging from 0.0000000000000000 through 0.9999999999999999 and assigns it to the variable **randomNumber**.

```
var randomNumber = Math.random();
```

The function always delivers a 16-place decimal that ranges from 0.0000000000000000 to 0.9999999999999999. We can convert the decimal to an integer by multiplying by one hundred quadrillion (1 followed by 16 zeroes):

0.0000000000000000 * 10000000000000000 = 0
0.7474887706339359 * 10000000000000000 = 7474887706339359
0.9999999999999999 * 10000000000000000 = 9999999999999999

Trillions of possible numbers are more than we need in our virtual die throw. We just want six possible numbers, 1 through 6. So instead of multiplying by a hundred quadrillion, our first step is to multiply the giant decimal by 6.

Here are three examples.

0.0000000000000000 * 6 = 0
0.7474887706339359 * 6 = 4.7474887706339359
0.9999999999999999 * 6 = 5.9999999999999994

Intuition may tell you that you can finish the job by rounding, but that doesn't work out mathematically. Because nothing rounds up to 0 and nothing rounds down to 6, the numbers in the middle, which are reached both by rounding up and rounding down, will come up almost twice as often. But we can give all the numbers an equal chance if we add 1 to the result, then round down. Here's the code for our virtual die throw.

```
1 var bigDecimal = Math.random();
2 var improvedNum = (bigDecimal * 6) + 1;
3 var numberOfStars = Math.floor(improvedNum);
```

This is what happens in the code above, line by line:

1. Generates a 16-place decimal and assigns it to the variable **bigDecimal**.

2. Converts the 16-place decimal to a number ranging from 0.0000000000000000 through 5.9999999999999999, then adds 1, so the range winds up 1.0000000000000000 through 6.9999999999999999. This number is assigned to the variable **improvedNum**.

3. Rounds the value represented by **improvedNum** down to the nearest integer that ranges from 1 through 6.

Find the interactive coding exercises for this chapter at http://www.ASmarterWayToLearn.com/js/27.html

28
Converting strings to integers and decimals

Sometimes JavaScript seems to read your mind. Suppose you write...

```
var currentAge = prompt("Enter your age.");
```

...JavaScript assigns the user's answer to **currentAge** as a string. Her entry, let's say 32, may look like a number to you, but to JavaScript it's a string: "32". Nevertheless, suppose you write...

```
1 var currentAge = prompt("Enter your age.");
2 var yearsEligibleToVote = currentAge - 18;
```

The value assigned to the variable **currentAge** is a string, because it comes from a user's *prompt* response. But in line 2, when the variable appears in an arithmetic expression, the value is automatically (and temporarily) converted to a number to make the math work.

Similarly, if you ask JavaScript to divide "100" by 2 or multiply "2.5" by 2.5, JavaScript seems to understand that you want the string treated as a number, and does the math. You can even ask JavaScript to multiply, divide, or subtract using nothing but strings as terms, and JavaScript, interpreting your intentions correctly, does the math.

```
var profit = "200" - "150";
```

In the statement above, the two strings are treated as numbers because they appear in a math expression. The variable **profit**, despite the quotation marks, is assigned the number 50. Of course, the string you ask JavaScript to do math on has to be a number contained in quotes, like "50", not letter characters. If you write...

```
var profit = "200" - "duck";
```

...an alert will display saying "NaN" meaning "not a number." No mystery here. How can 200 minus "duck" be a number?

You may recall from a previous chapter that when you mix strings and numbers in an expression involving a plus, JavaScript, rather than converting strings to numbers, JavaScript converts numbers to strings.

Rather than adding, it concatenates.

```
var result = "200" + 150;
```

In the statement above, JavaScript, seeing the string "200" and the number 150, resolves the conflict by converting 150 to a string: "150". Then it concatenates the two strings. The variable result is assigned "200150". If the **+** in the expression were one of the other arithmetic operators(**-**, *****, or **/**), JavaScript would convert the string "200" to the number 200 and do the math.

You can see there's going to be a problem with the following code.

```
1 var currentAge = prompt("Enter your age.");
2 var qualifyingAge = currentAge + 1;
```

The code above has an unintended consequence. The string represented by **currentAge** is concatenated with 1 that has been converted to "1". Example: if the user enters "52," **qualifyingAge** is assigned not 53 but "521".

If you want to do addition, you must convert any strings to numbers.

```
1 var currentAge = prompt("Enter your age.");
2 var qualifyingAge = parseInt(currentAge) + 1;
```

Line 2 converts the string represented by **currentAge** to a number before adding 1 to it and assigning the sum to **qualifyingAge**.

parseInt converts all strings, including strings comprising floating-point numbers, to integers. And shocking but true: It doesn't round. It simply lops off the decimals. In the following statement, **myInteger** is assigned not 2 as you might expect, but 1.

```
var myInteger = parseInt("1.9999");
```

To preserve any decimal values, use **parseFloat**. In the following statement **myFractional** is assigned 1.9999.

```
var myFractional = parseFloat("1.9999");
```

Find the interactive coding exercises for this chapter at
http://www.ASmarterWayToLearn.com/js/28.html

29
Converting strings to numbers, numbers to strings

In the last chapter you learned to use **parseInt** to convert a string representing a number into an integer. And you learned to use **parseFloat** to convert a string representing a number into a floating-point number. You can finesse the distinction between integers and floating-point numbers by using **Number**. This handy conversion tool converts a string representing either an integer or a floating-point number to a number that's identical to the one inside the parentheses. The following code converts the string "24" to the number 24.

```
1 var integerString = "24"
2 var num = Number(integerString);
```

The following code converts the string "24.9876" to the number 24.9876.

```
1 var floatingNumString = "24.9876";
2 var num = Number(floatingNumString);
```

Suppose your code has done an arithmetic calculation that yielded a number. Now you want to display the number as a string. This is how you do it.

```
1 var numberAsNumber = 1234;
2 var numberAsString = numberAsNumber.toString();
```

The code above converts the number 1234 to the string "1234" and assigns it to the variable **numberAsString**.

Find the interactive coding exercises for this chapter at http://www.ASmarterWayToLearn.com/js/29.html

30
Controlling the length of decimals

The price of the item is $9.95. The sales tax is 6.5% of the price. You combine the two numbers to get the total.

```
var total = price + (price * taxRate);
```

The variable **total** now has a value of 10.59675.

But that isn't what you're going to charge the customer, is it? You're going to charge her an amount rounded off to two decimal places: $10.60.

Here's how to do it.

```
var prettyTotal = total.toFixed(2);
```

The statement above rounds the number represented by **total** to 2 places and converts it to a string. It assigns the string to the variable **prettyTotal**. The number inside the parentheses tells JavaScript how many places to round the decimal to.

Now add a dollar sign, and you're all set.

```
var currencyTotal = "$" + prettyTotal;
```

To shorten a number to no decimals, leave the parentheses empty.

```
var prettyTotal = total.toFixed();
```

Unfortunately, the **toFixed** method comes with a surprise inside. If a decimal ends in 5, it usually rounds up, as you would expect. But, depending on the browser, sometimes it rounds down! If, for example, you apply the method to 1.555, specifying 2 decimal places, it may give you "1.56". Or it may produce "1.55".

There are sophisticated ways to address the problem. Here's an inelegant fix that uses methods you already know and understand.

```
1 var str = num.toString();
2 if (str.charAt(str.length - 1) === "5") {
3   str = str.slice(0, str.length - 1) + "6";
4 }
5 num = Number(str);
6 prettyNum = num.toFixed(2);
```

If the decimal ends in a 5, the code changes it to a 6 so the method is forced to round up when it should. Here's what's happening, line-by-line:

1. Converts the number to a string and assigns it to the variable `str`.

2. Checks to see if the last character is "5".

3. If so, slices off the "5" and appends "6".

4. --

5. Converts it back to a number.

6. Rounds it to 2 places.

Find the interactive coding exercises for this chapter at http://www.ASmarterWayToLearn.com/js/30.html

31
Getting the current date and time

Your webpage includes a notice telling the user the current local date and time in his particular time zone. But what is the current date and time? Here's how JavaScript finds out.

```javascript
var rightNow = new Date();
```

The statement above creates a *Date object*. This is what it looks like.

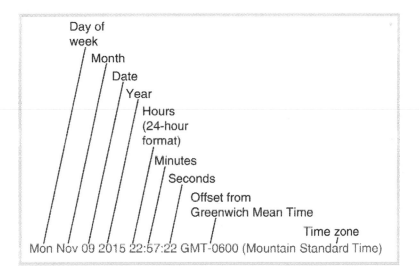

JavaScript gets this information from the user's computer. It is only as accurate as the computer's date and time settings. If the user has moved to a new time zone and hasn't reset the time zone on his computer, the computer will still be on the old time zone.

The Date object may resemble a string, but it isn't one. For example, you can't use methods on it like **charAt**, **indexOf**, or **slice**.

You can convert a Date object to a string the same way you convert a number to a string. Let's say you've created a Date object and assigned it to the variable **rightNow**. The following code converts it to a string and assigns the string to the variable **dateString**.

```javascript
var dateString = rightNow.toString();
```

The code above converts the Date object represented by the variable

rightNow to a string and assigns the string to the variable **dateString**. Most of the time, you'll just want to extract some of the information from the Date object without converting it to a string.

I'm going to show you how to extract the individual pieces of the Date object. In this chapter I'll get you started with the first piece. In the next chapter I'll cover the rest.

The following code creates a new Date object, assigns it to the variable **rightNow**, extracts the day of the week, and assigns the day of the week to the variable **theDay**.

```
1 var rightNow = new Date();
2 var theDay = rightNow.getDay();
```

In the diagram of the Date object that I showed you above, the day of the week was represented as "Mon." But when you extract the day of the week from the object, it's represented as a number. Days are designated by a number from 0 for Sunday through 6 for Saturday. This means that you'll need a bit of code to convert it back into a day name like "Mon."

```
1 var dayNames = ["Sun", "Mon", "Tue", "Wed", "Thu", "Fri",
"Sat"];
2 var now = new Date();
3 var theDay = now.getDay();
4 var nameOfToday = dayNames[theDay];
```

Here's what's going on:

1. Creates an array of days starting with "Sun" and assigns it to **dayNames**.

2. Creates a new Date object and assigns it to **now**.

3. Extracts the day of the week as a number and assigns it to **theDay**.

4. Uses the day number as an index to specify the correct array element, i.e. the day name.

Find the interactive coding exercises for this chapter at:
http://www.ASmarterWayToLearn.com/js/31.html

32
Extracting parts of the date and time

Here's a summary of important methods for extracting pieces of the Date object.

Method	Gets	Range	Example
getDay()	Day of week	0-6	0 is Sunday
getMonth()	Month	0-11	0 is January
getDate()	Day of month	1-31	1 is 1st of month
getFullYear()	Year		2015
getHours()	Hour	0-23	0 is midnight 12 is noon 23 is 11 p.m.
getMinutes()	Minute	0-59	
getSeconds()	Second	0-59	
getMilliseconds()	Milliseconds	0-999	
getTime()	Milliseconds since midnight, Jan. 1, 1970		

I covered **getDay** in the last chapter. Let's look at the rest of the extraction methods.

Like **getDay**, **getMonth** gives you not the spelled-out name of the month shown in the Date object, but a number. The following code produces a month number ranging from 0 for January through 11 for December.

```
1 var d = new Date();
2 var currentMonth = d.getMonth();
```

getDate gives you a number for the day of the month.

```
var dayOfMonth = d.getDate();
```

getFullYear gives you a 4-digit number for the year.

```
var currYr = d.getFullYear();
```

getHours gives you a number from 0 through 23 corresponding to midnight through 11 p.m.

```
var currentHrs = d.getHours();
```

getMinutes gives you a number from 0 through 59.

```
var currMins = d.getMinutes();
```

getSeconds gives you a number from 0 through 59.

```
var currSecs = d.getSeconds();
```

getMilliseconds gives you a number from 0 through 999.

```
var currMills = d.getMilliseconds();
```

getTime gives you the number of milliseconds that have elapsed since midnight, Jan. 1, 1970.

```
var millsSince = d.getTime();
```

Find the interactive coding exercises for this chapter athttp://www.ASmarterWayToLearn.com/js/32.html

33
Specifying a date and time

How many days before the U.S. Social Security program goes broke?

Let's start with the estimated date. According to the system's trustees, the money will run out in 2035. They didn't pin down an exact date. Let's pick the middle of the year—June 30.

Okay, that's the hard part—pinpointing doomsday. Once we have that, constructing a day-by-day countdown is a JavaScript romp.

You already know how to do the first step, creating a Date object for the current date and time:

```
1 var today = new Date();
```

Next, you create a second Date object. But this time you specify the future date, June 30, 2035.

```
2 var doomsday = new Date("June 30, 2035");
```

Notice how the date is specified. It's in quotes. The month is spelled out. There's a comma after the day of the month. The year is expressed in four digits.

Next, you extract from both dates the milliseconds that have elapsed since the reference date of January 1, 1970.

```
3 var msToday = today.getTime();
4 var msDoomsday = doomsday.getTime();
```

You calculate the difference.

```
5 var msDiff = msDoomsday - msToday;
```

Some simple math converts the milliseconds to days.

```
6 var dDiff = msDiff / (1000 * 60 * 60 * 24);
```

The huge number created by the math inside the parentheses converts the milliseconds into seconds (1000), minutes (60), hours (60), and days (24).

You want a number that represents whole days, so you round down.

The following statement rounds the number of days, which is probably a number with decimal value, down to an integer.

```
7 dDiff = Math.floor(dDiff);
```

Here's the whole thing, condensed into something that looks more like production code

```
1 var msDiff = new Date("June 30, 2035").getTime() - new
Date().getTime();
2 var daysTillDoom = Math.floor(msDiff / (1000 * 60 * 60 *
24));
```

Line 1 subtracts the milliseconds since the reference date of the current moment from the milliseconds since the reference date of June 30, 2035. Line 2 converts the milliseconds to days and rounds down.

If the time is important, you can specify that as well.

```
var d = new Date("July 21, 1983 13:25:00");
```

Note the form used to specify the time: No comma after the date. 24-hour time. Colons separating hours, minutes, and seconds.

Find the interactive coding exercises for this chapter athttp://www.ASmarterWayToLearn.com/js/33.html

34
Changing elements of a date and time

You can change individual elements of a Date object. Here's a summary:

Method	Example (variable representing the Date object is d)	Result
setFullYear ()	d.setFullYear(2006)	Year is 2006
setMonth ()	d.setMonth(6)	Month is 6 (July)
setDate ()	d.setDate(6)	Day of the month is 6
setHours ()	d.setHours(6)	6 a.m.
setMinutes ()	d.setMinutes(6)	6 minutes past the hour
setSeconds ()	d.setSeconds(6)	6 seconds past the minute
setMilliseconds ()	d.setMilliseconds(6)	6 milliseconds past the second

setFullYear sets the year of an existing Date object without changing any other element.

```
1 var d = new Date();
2 d.setFullYear(2001);
```

Line 1 creates a new Date object for the current moment. Line 2 changes the year of the Date object to 2001, leaving all other elements of the Date object intact.

setMonth sets the month of an existing Date object without changing any other element.

```
1 var d = new Date();
2 d.setMonth(11);
```

Line 1 creates a new Date object for the current moment. Line 2 changes the month of the Date object to 11 (December), leaving all other elements of the Date object intact.

setDate sets the day of the month of an existing Date object without changing any other element.

```
1 var d = new Date();
2 d.setDate(15);
```

Line 1 creates a new Date object for the current moment. Line 2 changes the date of the Date object to the 15th of the month, leaving all other elements of the Date object intact.

setHours sets the hours of an existing Date object without changing any other element.

```
1 var d = new Date();
2 d.setHours(13);
```

Line 1 creates a new Date object for the current moment. Line 2 changes the hours of the Date object to the 13th hour (1 p.m.), leaving all other elements of the Date object intact.

setMinutes sets the minutes of an existing Date object without changing any other element.

```
1 var d = new Date();
2 d.setMinutes(05);
```

Line 1 creates a new Date object for the current moment. Line 2 changes the minutes of the Date object to 5 minutes after the hour, leaving all other elements of the Date object intact.

setSeconds sets the seconds of an existing Date object without changing any other element.

```
1 var d = new Date();
2 d.setSeconds(55);
```

Line 1 creates a new Date object for the current moment. Line 2 changes the seconds of the Date object to the 55 seconds after the minute, leaving all other elements of the Date object intact.

setMilliseconds sets the milliseconds of an existing Date object without changing any other element.

```
1 var d = new Date();
2 d.setMilliseconds(867);
```

Line 1 creates a new Date object for the current moment. Line 2 changes the milliseconds of the Date object to 867 milliseconds after the second, leaving all other elements of the Date object intact.

Find the interactive coding exercises for this chapter at http://www.ASmarterWayToLearn.com/js/34.html

35
Functions

A *function* is a block of JavaScript that robotically does the same thing again and again, whenever you invoke its name. It saves you repetitive coding and makes your code easier to understand.

On your website, suppose there are several pages where you want to display an alert that tells the user the current time. (To keep it simple, we'll settle for 24-hour time rather than converting to a.m. and p.m.) The code might look like this.

```
1 var now = new Date();
2 var theHr = now.getHours();
3 var theMin = now.getMinutes();
4 alert("time: " + theHr + ":" + theMin);
```

You could write this block of code over and over again, every time you need it. Or you could write it once as a function, naming it, say, **tellTime**. After that, this is the only code you'll need in order to make the whole block execute:

```
tellTime();
```

Whenever JavaScript sees that short statement, the time-telling block executes.

This is how you package the one-off code above as a repeatable function:

```
1 function tellTime() {
2    var now = new Date();
3    var theHr = now.getHours();
4    var theMin = now.getMinutes();
5    alert("Current time: "+ theHr + ":" + theMin);
6 }
```

The time-telling code—the code that creates the Date object, extracts the time, formats it, and displays an alert—is exactly the same code we started with, but is now packaged as a function. Here are the parts:

On line 1 an opening declaration statement that includes:

- the keyword **function**

- a name I made up for the function

- parentheses that identify it as a function

- an opening curly bracket to enclose the code that will execute

On lines 2 through 5 the same block of code that you saw before executes, but it's indented for clarity. Opinions vary on how much to indent. I train you to indent 2 spaces.

On line 6 a closing curly bracket on its own line encloses the code that will execute.

Again, note that the *calling code*—the code that invokes the function—does nothing more than state the name of the function including its parentheses.

```
tellTime();
```

You can give a function any name that would be a legal variable name, then add parentheses. Function-naming follows the same rules as variable naming because, technically, a function is a variable. This will make more sense to you when you learn more about functions in a subsequent chapter.

Functions and the statements that call them may be separated by thousands of lines of code. Typically, functions are in the same place as the main code—in an external JavaScript file, at the end of the HTML body section, or in the HTML head section. Normally, all the functions should precede the main code, so when they're called by the main code, they're already loaded in memory and ready to go.

Find the interactive coding exercises for this chapter at http://www.ASmarterWayToLearn.com/js/35.html

36
Functions: Passing them data

A function is a block of code that does something robotically, whenever you invoke its name. For example, when you write **greetUser();** a function with that name executes. To be clear: The kind of function I'm talking about is one that you've written yourself, and named yourself.

Suppose that when you write **greetUser();** a function is called that displays an alert saying, "Hello, there."

This is the code for the function.

```
1 function greetUser() {
2    alert("Hello, there.");
3 }
```

One of the really useful things about functions is that those parentheses in the calling code don't have to be empty. If you put some data inside the parentheses, you can pass that data to the function that it'll use when it executes.

Suppose, instead of writing **greetUser();** you write...

```
greetUser("Hello, there.");
```

Now, instead of just calling the function, you're calling it and *passing data* to it. The string inside the parentheses, i.e. the data you're passing, is called an *argument*.

The function is now more versatile, because the message it displays is no longer hard-wired into it. It'll display any message that you pass to it from the calling code, via the argument.

In order for a function to become a programmable robot rather than a one-job robot, you have to set it up to receive the data you're passing. Here's how you do it.

```
1 function greetUser(greeting) {
2    alert(greeting);
3 }
```

So now we've filled the parentheses of both the calling code and the function definition. The parentheses of the calling code contain an argument. In the example, the argument is the string "Hello, there." And, as you can see in the example above, the parentheses of the function definition now contain a variable, **greeting**.

A variable inside the parentheses in a function statement is known as a *parameter*. The parameter name is up to you. You can give it any name that would be legal for a variable. Then you can use it to accomplish something in the body of the function. On line 2 in the example above, I used it to specify the message in an alert.

You don't have to declare a variable when it's used as a parameter in a function definition. When it's used as a parameter, the declaration is implicit.

The argument in the statement that calls the function —"Hello, there."—is the data that's passed to the function. The parameter inside the parentheses in the function definition catches the data that's passed. It now holds "Hello, there." In other words, the string "Hello, there", specified in the function call, is assigned to **greeting** in the function. Then that variable, **greeting**, is used to specify the message in the alert statement.

The value passed to a function is used in the body of the function to accomplish something. In this case, the value is used to specify the message in the alert.

In the example, the argument is a string, but it could just as easily be a variable. In the following code, I declare the variable **greeting** and assign it the value "Hello, there." Then, rather than using the string itself as an argument in the function call, I use the variable.

```
1 var greeting = "Hello, there."
2 greetUser(greeting);
```

In the example above, the name of the function **greetUser**, shares some of its name with the parameter **greeting**, but that's just to make the code easy to understand. The name of the function and the name of the parameter don't have to have anything in common. And remember, these names are up to you, as long as you follow the variable-naming rules.

In the example, I named the argument in the calling code **greeting**, and also named the parameter in the function code **greeting**. But this isn't necessary, either. They don't have to match.

No matter what an argument's name is, it is accepted by the parameter, no matter what the parameter's name is. In the following code, the variable **whatever** is the argument. The parameter **greeting** doesn't match the name, but still catches the value.

Here's the function, once again, with the parameter **greeting**.

```
1 function greetUser(greeting) {

2   alert(greeting);

3 }
```

And here's the statement that calls the function, with the argument **whatever**.

```
1 var whatever = "Hello, there.";
2 greetUser(whatever);
```

It's okay that the name of the argument and the name of the parameter don't match. The parameter still catches the argument, the string "Hello, there."

Still, it often makes sense to give an argument and a parameter the same name, for clarity.

A number, either a literal number or a number represented by a variable, can be an argument. In the following code I declare the variable **almostAMil** and assign the number 999999 to it. Then I use **almostAMil** as the argument in the function call.

```
1 var almostAMil = 999999;
2 showBigNum(almostAMil);
```

Alternatively, if I wanted to, I could use the literal number 999999 as the argument.

```
showBigNum(999999);
```

You can pass any number of arguments, separated by commas, to a function. Typically, the function has the same number of parameters, also separated by commas. (There are rare exceptions for special cases.) Again, when you use variables as arguments, their names don't have to match the names of the parameters. JavaScript matches up arguments and parameters according to their order, not their names. The first argument in the list is passed to the first parameter in the list, the second argument is passed to the second parameter, and so on.

As arguments, you can use any combination of variables, strings, and literal numbers. In the following example, the calling code passes a variable, a string, and a number to the function. Three parameters catch the values. The function concatenates them to create an alert message.

First, here's the function.

```
1 function showMessage(m, string, num) {
2    alert(m + string + num);
3 }
```

Now here's the statement that calls the function.

```
1 var month = "March";
2 showMessage(month, "'s winning number is ", 23);
```

The argument, **month**, a variable, is passed to the parameter **m**. The argument "'s winning number is ", a string, is passed to the parameter string. The argument 23, a literal number, is passed to the parameter **num**.

When the code executes, an alert displays saying, "March's winning number is 23."

Normally, you'd use all the parameters included in the function definition as variables in the code that executes, because, why else would you want them in the function definition? But there's nothing that says you must use them all. And you certainly don't have to use them in the same order in which they appear within the parentheses. Each one is a full-fledged variable that, within the function, you can use the way you'd use any variable.

Find the interactive coding exercises for this chapter at http://www.ASmarterWayToLearn.com/js/36.html

37
Functions: Passing data back from them

As you learned in the last chapter, a function becomes more versatile when you pass data to it so it can deliver a custom job.

But a function can do even more. It can pass data *back* to the calling code.

Let's say you charge a minimum shipping rate of $5, plus 3 percent of the merchandise total above $50, up to $100. You offer free shipping when the total hits $100. Here's the code that calculates the order total.

```
1  var orderTot;
2  if (merchTot >= 100) {
3    orderTot = merchTot;"
4  }
5  else if (merchTot < 50.01) {
6    orderTot = merchTot + 5;
7  }
8  else {
9    orderTot = merchTot + 5 + (.03 * (merchTot - 50));
10 }
```

If the merchandise total is at least $100 (line 2), the order total is the same as the merchandise total (line 3). If the merchandise total is $50 or less (line 5), the order total is the merchandise total plus $5 (line 6). If the order total is between $50 and $100 (line 8), the order total is the merchandise total plus $5 plus 3 percent of the amount over $50 (line 9).

Something costing $150 is $150 total.

Something costing $15 is $20 total.

Something costing $70 is $75.60 total.

Here's how we turn the code above into a function.

```
1   function calcTot(merchTot) {
2      var orderTot;
3      if (merchTot >= 100) {
4         orderTot = merchTot;
5      }
6      else if (merchTot < 50.01) {
7         orderTot = merchTot + 5;
8      }
9      else {
10        orderTot = merchTot + 5 + (.03 * (merchTot - 50));
11     }
12     return orderTot;

13 }
```

The thing to focus on here is that we declare a variable, **orderTot** (line 2), and then—here's what's new—after the processing is done and the merchandise total is known, the function *returns* the value held in **orderTot** to the calling code (line 12). It passes data *back*.

But then the calling code needs something to catch the data. What else could this something be but a variable? Here's the code that calls the function.

```
var totalToCharge = calcTot(79.99);
```

If you're new to coding, this statement may look odd to you. How can a function be assigned to a variable? You may be used to seeing a literal value assigned to a variable....

```
var totalToCharge = 85.00;
```

You may be used to seeing a variable assigned to a variable...

```
var totalToCharge = merchTotal;
```

And you may be used to seeing an arithmetic or other expression assigned to a variable...

```
var totalToCharge = merchTotal + ship + tax;
```

But assigning a function to a variable?

Well, it's not really that odd, because, remember, what you're actually assigning to the variable is the value passed back by the **return** statement in the function code. The statement...

106

```
var totalToCharge = calcTot(79.99);
```

...is shorthand for: "Assign to the variable **totalToCharge** the value returned by the function **calcTot**."

So now there's two-way communication between the calling code and the function. The calling code passes the value 79.99 to the function, which is caught by the function's parameter **merchTot**. This variable, **merchTot**, is used in the body of the function to calculate an order total. Then, through the **return** statement, that order total is passed back to **totalToCharge** in the calling code. It's a complete circle.

Notice that the variable in the calling code, **totalToCharge**, that catches the value is different from the variable inside the function, **merchTot**, that returns the value. I did this purposely, so you wouldn't think the two variables have to share the same name. In the last chapter you learned that when an argument in the calling code passes a value to a parameter in the function definition, they can have the same name, but don't have to. The same applies to the variable that's returned from a function and the variable in the calling code that catches it. They can share the same name, but don't have to.

Anywhere you can use a variable, you can use a function. (Technically, a function *is* a variable.) For example...

You can use a function to specify the message in an alert.

```
alert(calcTot(79.99));
```

In the example above, the alert message is the value returned by the function **calcTot** when the function is passed 79.99 as a parameter.

You can use a function in an expression.

```
var orderTot = merchTot + calcTax(merchTot);
```

In the example above, the value assigned to **orderTot** is the sum of **merchTot** and the value returned by the function **calcTax** when the function is passed **merchTot** as an argument.

You can use a function in a function call.

```
var tot = calc(merchTot, calcTax(merchTot));
```

In the example above, the calling code passes two arguments to the function **calc**. The first argument is **merchTot**. The second argument is the function **calcTax**, which is also passed **merchTot**.

Within a function, you can call another function.

```
1 function calcTot(price) {
2   return price + calcShip(price);
3 }
```

In the example above, the function **calcTot** calls the function **calcShip**. It passes **price** as an argument and receives the shipping charge back. It adds the shipping charge to the price, and returns the sum to the original calling code as a total.

You've learned that you can pass any number of arguments to any number of parameters. Unfortunately, you don't have this flexibility in the **return** statement. No matter how many parameters it takes or how much processing it does, a function can return only a single value to the code that calls it.

Find the interactive coding exercises for this chapter at http://www.ASmarterWayToLearn.com/js/37.html

38
Functions: Local vs. global variables

Now we come to the subject of variable *scope*. That is, the difference between *global* and *local* variables. Some variables have global scope, which makes them global variables. Other variables have local scope, which makes them local variables. Nothing could be simpler, but for some reason, when the subject comes up in books and tutorials, obfuscation often rules. Relax. This will be easy.

A global variable is one that's declared in the main body of your code—that is, *not* inside a function.

A local variable is one that's declared inside a function. It can be either a parameter of the function, which is declared implicitly by being named as a parameter, or a variable declared explicitly in the function with the **var** keyword.

What makes a global variable global is that it is meaningful in every section of your code, whether that code is in the main body or in any of the functions. Global scope is like global fame. Wherever you go in the world, they've heard of Bill Clinton. A local variable is one that's meaningful only within the function that declares it. Local scope is like local fame. The mayor of Duluth is known only in Duluth.

So there are two differences between global and local variables—where they're declared, and where they're known and can be used.

Global variables	Local variables
Declared in the main code	Declared in a function
Known everywhere, useable everywhere	Known only inside the function, useable only inside the function

Before I show you the first example, I want you to set aside what you know about passing values to a function through arguments, and passing a value back to the calling code by way of the return statement. Pretend you don't know anything about these things. I'll come back to them later. Here's an example.

The main code declares a variable and calls a function:

```
1 var theSum;
2 addNumbers();
```

Then the function:

```
1 function addNumbers() {
2    theSum = 2 + 2;
3 }
```

In the example, the variable **theSum** is declared in the main code. The function **addNumbers** is called to assign it a value. Having been declared in the main code, the variable has global scope, so this function or any other function can use it. So can anything in the main code. The function assigns the sum of 2 + 2 to this global variable. Since the variable has global scope, the assignment is meaningful in all sections of your code, both the main code and in all functions. The variable has the value 4 in the function **addNumbers**, in the main code, and in any other functions that use it. When I write...

```
alert(theSum);
```

...whether I write it in the main code, in the function **addNumbers**, or in any other function, an alert will display the number 4.

But if I declare the variable inside the function...

```
1 function addNumbers() {
2    var theSum = 2 + 2;
3 }
```

...the variable has the value 4 only inside the function. Everywhere else, it's unknown. Everywhere else, it has no value at all. Since the variable **theSum** is declared with the keyword **var** inside the function, not in the main code, its scope is local. It is meaningful only inside the function. In other functions and in the main code, it is unknown. If I write...

```
alert(theSum);
```

...in the function, an alert displays the number 4, because the variable **theSum** is known inside the function, where it was declared. But if I write the same alert statement anywhere else—in the main code or in another function—the code breaks, because **theSum** is unknown

110

outside the function.

Note: I say that a variable has local scope when you declare it in a function. By "declaring it in a function" I mean that you declare the variable explicitly with the keyword **var**—as opposed to casually introducing it into the function without **var**. (The exception is if you name it as a parameter, in which case it's declared implicitly as a local variable of the function.) If you get sloppy and begin using a new variable in the body of a function without explicitly declaring it in the function with the keyword **var**, it is global—even though you haven't declared it anywhere in the main code.

Now, to illustrate a point, I'm going to do something you'd actually never want to do in your code. I'm going to declare a variable both in the main code and in the function.

First, in the main code:

```
1 var theSum = 1000;
2 addNumbers();
```

Then in the function:

```
1 function addNumbers() {
2     var theSum = 2 + 2;
3 }
```

By declaring the variable twice—once in the main code and again in the function—I've created *two different variables* that share the same name. One **theSum** is global. The other **theSum** is local. This is not something you would ever want to do—it sets you up for coding mistakes and makes your code almost impossible to follow—but I did it to show the difference between global and local scope. By declaring **theSum** once in the main code, and again in the function, I've created (1) a global variable that's useable *almost* everywhere and (2) a local variable of the same name that's useable only inside the function. Why do I say the global variable is useable *almost* everywhere? Because it's no good inside the function. Inside the function, the name **theSum** stands for a local variable, so the name can't refer to the global variable. In this situation, coders say the global variable is *in the shadow of* the local variable. Inside the function, it can't be seen. Inside the function, only the local variable of that name can be seen.

The local variable **theSum** has a value of 4 inside the function, but

theSum outside the function has a value of 1000.

Now let's journey a little farther into Wonderland, Alice.

First, a statement in the main code:

```
1  var theSum = addNumbers();
```

Then a function:

```
1  function addNumbers() {
2     var theSum = 2 + 2;
3     return theSum;
4  }
```

Again, this isn't something you'd actually code. I use the example only to demonstrate principles. In this code, you still have two different variables—a global variable and a local variable—that share the same name, **theSum**, but now, thanks to the **return** statement, the value of the local variable is assigned to the global variable. Now both variables have the same name and the same value, but they're still different variables.

Which brings us to a question you may be asking:

If a function can use a global variable, why do you have to pass a value from an argument to a parameter? Why not just declare a global variable, then have the function use it? Well, you can, but asking functions to work with global variables is asking them to eavesdrop on the main code, and like human eavesdropping, it invites mischief in the form of confusion and unintended consequences. There is no controversy among coders about this. It's always best to pass values explicitly to functions through arguments. Global variables have no place in functions.

The same logic applies to the argument for using the **return** statement. You can change the value of a global variable within a function. When you do, the value of it changes everywhere, including in the main code. No **return** is needed. But it's better practice to use a local variable within the function, then pass that value back explicitly through a **return** statement.

Find the interactive coding exercises for this chapter at:
http://www.ASmarterWayToLearn.com/js/38.html

39
switch statements: How to start them

Consider this chain of conditional statements.

```
1 if (dayOfWk === "Sat" || dayOfWk === "Sun") {
2   alert("Whoopee!");
3 }
4 else if (dayOfWk === "Fri") {
5   alert("TGIF!");
6 }
7 else {
8   alert("Shoot me now!");
9 }
```

If it's a weekend day, the "Whoopee!" alert displays. If it's Friday, the "TGIF" alert displays. If it's a weekday, the "Shoot me now" alert displays.

It works, but it's unwieldy and a little ugly, especially if you have many conditions to test. It's time for you to learn a more elegant alternative that you can use for testing myriad conditions, the *switch* statement. The more conditions you need to test, the more you'll like the *switch* statement. This *switch* statement duplicates the functionality of the example above.

```
1  switch(dayOfWk) {
2  case "Sat" :
3    alert("Whoopee");
4    break;
5  case "Sun" :
6    alert("Whoopee");
7    break;
8  case "Fri" :
9    alert("TGIF!");
10   break;
11 default :
12   alert("Shoot me now!");
13 }
```

For the moment, I want you to focus on just the first three lines of the code above.

1. Begins with the keyword **switch**. Bumping up against it is the variable that's being tested, inside parentheses. Then there's an opening curly bracket.

2. The first possibility, that the variable **dayOfWeek** has the value "Sat". Begins with the keyword **case**. Then the value that is being tried, "Sat". Then a space and a colon.

3. The statement that executes if the test passes—if **dayOfWeek** does, in fact, have the value "Sat". This statement is indented. Any number of statements can execute if the test passes.

Find the interactive coding exercises for this chapter at http://www.ASmarterWayToLearn.com/js/39.html

40
switch statements: How to complete them

In the last chapter you focused on the first three lines of this *switch* statement.

```
1  switch(dayOfWk) {
2  case "Sat" :
3    alert("Whoopee");
4    break;
5  case "Sun" :
6    alert("Whoopee");
7    break;
8  case "Fri" :
9    alert("TGIF!");
10   break;
11 default :
12   alert("Shoot me now!");
13 }
```

In this chapter you'll tackle the rest of the code.

The first line of an *if* statement is followed by a statement (or statements) that executes if the condition is true. A *switch* statement works similarly. On the line below each **case** clause, there's a statement (or statements) that executes if the case is true.

Once again, the code that executes if the case is true is indented 2 spaces. (The universal convention is that it is indented by some amount. Opinions differ on how much is best. I standardize on a 2-space indentation, which is common but far from universal.)

But why do all of the cases except the last one include a **break** statement?

JavaScript has an inconvenient quirk: After a true case is found, JavaScript not only executes the statement(s) immediately below that case. It executes all the statements for all the cases below it. So after a true case is found and the conditional code executes, you need to jump out of the **switch** block by coding a **break** statement. If, for example, you omit the **break** statements in the code above, this happens:

An alert displays saying "Whoopee!"
A second alert displays saying "Whoopee!"
A third alert displays saying "TGIF!"
A fourth alert displays saying "Shoot me now."
Now let's look at line 11.

```
11 default :
12    alert("Shoot me now!");
13 }
```

The keyword **default** works like **else** in an *if...else* statement. The code that follows it executes if none of the conditions above it are met. So, in the example above, if **dayOfWk** isn't "Sat" or "Sun" or "Fri"—if it's anything other than those three values—an alert displays saying "Shoot me now."

Note that **default** is followed by a space and a colon, just like the **case** clauses above it.

Note also that there's no **break** statement. That's because **default** always comes last, which means there are no statements below it to execute inappropriately.

In a *switch* statement, **default** code is optional, just as **else** code is optional after an *if* statement. Without the **default** code, if none of the cases test true, nothing happens.

When there is no **default** code, careful coders include a **break** statement after the last condition anyway as insurance, even though it may be superfluous. If you decide to add a new condition to the end later, you won't have to remember to add a **break** to the block above it in order to avoid a disastrous cascade of statements.

Find the interactive coding exercises for this chapter at: http://www.ASmarterWayToLearn.com/js/40.html

41
while loops

This *for* loop displays an alert on each iteration.

```
1 for (var i = 0; i <= 3; i++) {
2 alert(i);
3 }
```

As you know, the process is controlled by the three terms inside the parentheses:

var i = 0 establishes a counter.

i <= 3 says the loop is to keep running as long as **i** is less than or equal to 3. Since **i** is assigned 0 initially, the loop will run 4 times.

i++ increments **i** on each iteration.

All the how-to-loop directions are packed into the space between the parentheses: where to start the counter, how long to keep the loop going, and how to update the counter each time through.

A *while* loop does the same thing, but it's organized differently. Only the middle term, how long to keep the loop going, is inside the parentheses. The counter is defined before the first line of the *while* block. The counter is updated within the code that executes when the loop runs.

```
1 var i = 0;
2 while (i <= 3) {
3   alert(i);
4   i++;
5 }
```

In other ways, a *while* loop is organized along the same lines as a for loop.

- Parentheses enclose the loop limiter.

- Curly brackets enclose the code that executes.

- The code that executes is indented 2 spaces.

Since any *for* loop can be translated into a *while* loop and vice versa, you can use whichever one you prefer.

Find the interactive coding exercises for this chapter at http://www.ASmarterWayToLearn.com/js/41.html

42
do...while loops

In a *while* loop the order of instructions is:

1. Declare a variable to serve as a counter, and assign a value to it.

2. Start the loop, specifying how long the loop is to run.

3. Execute one or more statements.

4. Within the loop, as a final statement, advance the counter.

```
1 var i = 0;
2 while (i <= 3) {
3   alert(i);
4   i++;
5 }
```

A *do...while* loop accomplishes almost the same task as a *while* loop.

```
1 var i = 0;
2 do {
3   alert(i);
4   i++;
5 } while (i <= 3);
```

The differences between the two types of loops:

- Instead of **while**, the keyword **do** leads off the statement.

- The *while* clause, including the loop-limiting code inside the parentheses, moves to the bottom—after the closing curly bracket.

Note that the *while* clause ends with a semicolon.

Functionally, the difference between a *while* loop and a *do...while* loop is that it's possible to code a *while* statement whose block of instructions never execute. Consider this *while* loop.

```
1 var i = 0;
2 while (i < 0) {
3    alert(i);
4    i++;
5 }
```

The code says to keep running an alert as long as the counter is less than 0. But since the counter is never less than 0, the code inside the curly brackets never executes.

Compare this with the *do...while* loop.

```
1 var i = 0;
2 do {
3    alert(i);
4    i++;
5 } while (i < 0);
```

The alert will display once, even though the keep-going condition—**i** less than 0—never occurs. Since a *do...while* loop executes the code inside the curly brackets before it gets to the loop-limiter at the bottom, it always executes that code at least once, no matter what the loop-limiter says.

Find the interactive coding exercises for this chapter at http://www.ASmarterWayToLearn.com/js/42.html

43
Placing scripts

JavaScript code doesn't care where it lives. It can be mixed in with—that is, *embedded* in—the HTML that creates a Web page. Or, like an external CSS file, it can be placed in a separate file that is loaded by the HTML file. In most cases, it's best to have an external JavaScript file, for some of the same reasons it's best to have an external CSS file. But it's still good to know how to place JavaScript within your HTML file, so let's start with that.

As you know, the order of HTML code is important, because it determines the order of elements on the page. If you want the heading to appear above the text, you put the heading above the text in the HTML. But JavaScript doesn't work the same way. All of your JavaScript functions, for example, are loaded into memory when the page loads. Wherever the code may be, the browser finds it and stores it by the time the page is finished loading. Once the page is loaded, all the JavaScript code stays in memory, ready to execute, for as long as the page is displayed.

You can legally put JavaScript code almost anywhere in the HTML file—in the head section, at the beginning of the body section, somewhere in the middle of the body section, or at the end of the body section. You could, if you wanted to be perverse, sprinkle different Javascript functions all over your HTML file in different places. The browser would sort it all out.

Generally, the best place for scripts, though, is at the end of the body section. This guarantees that CSS styling and image display won't get held up while scripts are loading.

When you embed blocks of JavaScript in HTML (as opposed to having a separate JavaScript file), you must enclose the JavaScript code between **\<script>** and **\</script>** tags. Here are two functions enclosed between the tags.

```
1 <script>
2 function sayHi() {
3   alert("Hello world!");
4 }
5 function sayBye() {
6   alert("Buh-bye!");
7 }
8 </script>
```

You can enclose any amount of code—including any number of functions—between the **<script>** and **</script>** tags. And, as I mentioned before, you can have different sections of code scattered all over your HTML file if you want. But each section has to be enclosed between **<script>** and **</script>** tags.

For most purposes, coders prefer to have all or most of their JavaScript code in a separate JavaScript file, then have the browser load this external file at the same time it's loading the HTML file.

A JavaScript file is, like HTML and CSS files, a simple text file. It doesn't have a header or any other special sections. It doesn't even have **<script>** and **</script>** tags. It's just pure JavaScript code. The entire contents of a JavaScript file that holds the two functions in the example above would be:

```
1 function sayHi() {
2   alert("Hello world!");
3 }
4 function sayBye() {
5   alert("Buh-bye!");
6 }
```

What makes a JavaScript file a JavaScript file is its file extension: **.js**. The front end of the file name is up to you, as long as it's legal. For example, any of these would be fine.

- scripts.js

- coreJS.js

- main-code.js

- main_code.js

- main.code.js

You include a JavaScript file in an HTML file the same way you include an external CSS file—with an opening and closing tag.

```
<script src="whatever.js"></script>
```

For the same reason that it's a good idea to put JavaScript code at the end of the body section, it's a good idea to place the markup that includes JavaScript files at the end of the body section.

You can include as many external JavaScript files as you like.

You can include JavaScript files and also embed other JavaScript code in the HTML.

Find the interactive coding exercises for this chapter at http://www.ASmarterWayToLearn.com/js/43.html

44
Commenting

Commenting, as you know if you have previous experience with HTML and CSS or other computer languages, is a way to tell the browser to ignore certain portions of text that you include within the body of code. Comments are for the human, not the machine. They help you and others understand your code when it comes time to revise. You can also use commenting to *comment out* portions of your code for testing and debugging. Since, compared with HTML or CSS, JavaScript is typically harder to understand when you come back to it later, you may want to put extra effort into commenting your JS code, especially if you're working in a team or if someone else may be asked to maintain your code in the future.

In HTML there's only one way to mark text as a comment. You write **<!--** to open and **-->** to close. And in CSS there's only one way to mark text as a comment. You write **/*** to open and ***/** to close. But in Javascript there are two ways mark text as a comment.

The first way is to mark a single line as a comment, as in line 1 here.

```
1  // This is a comment, ignored by the browser
2  for (var i = 0; i < animals.length; i++) {
3    if (animals[i] === "bat") {
4      animals[i] = "cat";
5    }
6  }
```

The two slashes mean, "Everything from here to the end of this line is a comment." In the example above, that means the whole line is a comment, since the slashes are at the beginning. But you can write a line that's part-code and part-comment, this way.

```
var animals = []; // Declare an empty array
```

You can write as many lines of comments as you like. Every line must begin with the two slashes.

```
// Each comment line must begin with a pair
// of slashes, like this. (Most code editors,
// by the way, are smart enough to recognize
// comments and render them in a different
// color so they're easy for you to
// distinguish from code.)
```

When you comment with slashes, there's no closing tag, because the end of the line closes the comment automatically.

For legibility, separate the pair of slashes from the comment with a space. When you're combining code with a comment on the same line, separate the code from the pair of slashes with a space.

When a comment requires more than one line, many coders prefer an alternative method, the *block comment*. If you use CSS, you're already familiar with these tags.

```
When a comment requires more than one line,
a block comment like this, with its opening
and closing tags, is the way to go.
*/
```

JavaScript block comment tags are the same as CSS comment tags. Open with **/***. Close with ***/**.

Find the interactive coding exercises for this chapter at http://www.ASmarterWayToLearn.com/js/44.html

45
Events: link

A good website is an interactive website. The user does something—clicks a button, moves the mouse, presses a key—and something happens. JavaScript gives you many ways to respond to the user's needs. A few examples:

The user clicks a button saying "Our Guarantee" and an alert displays spelling out the guarantee.

A page displays a "before" picture of a model. When the user mouses over the picture, it is replaced by an "after" picture of her.

The user types a number in the Ounces field on a form. When she clicks in the Grams field, the equivalent in grams displays.

The user has entered her email address in a form, and is about to type a comment. When she moves the cursor from the email field to the comment field, JavaScript checks to see if the email address is valid. In this case, it isn't—she's omitted ".com" at the end of the address. A message displays letting her know that she's entered an invalid email address.

On an online shopping site, there's a picture of a black watch. Next to it is a drop-down list asking the user to choose a color. When she chooses, the color of the watch in the picture changes to that color.

All of these user actions—clicking a button, moving the mouse, moving from one field to another in a form, selecting a different option—are known as *events*. JavaScript code that responds to an event—for example, displaying a guarantee or swapping an image when the pointer hovers over it—is called an *event handler*.

In this chapter and the ones that immediately follow, you'll learn the oldest and most straightforward approach to event-handling—*inline* event-handling. When you're writing production code, this is not the best way to handle events, for the same reason that inline CSS styling isn't the best way to format HTML elements. But since it's the least abstract way to do it, it's the easiest to learn, and can serve as a stepping stone to more advanced methods. Later in the book, you'll learn the approach that's preferred by most professionals—the *scripting* approach.

Inline event-handling means that you combine bits of JavaScript with HTML markup. Here's a line that displays a link and then displays an alert when the user clicks it.

```
<a href="#" onClick="alert('Hi');">Click</a>
```

As an HTML coder, you're familiar with the beginning and end of this markup, **<a href=** and **>Click</a>**

But when the user clicks this link, it behaves differently than normal hyperlinks. Instead of taking the user to another page, or to a named anchor on the same page, it displays an alert saying "Hi".

When the user clicks the link, it goes nowhere, and instead executes a JavaScript statement, in this case calling a function.

Let's break it down.

- When the user clicks the link, you don't want a new webpage to be loaded in this case, so, instead of a URL, you place a **#** inside the quotation marks. This tells the browser to reload the current page.

- **onClick=** says, "When the button is clicked, execute the following JavaScript." **onClick** isn't case-sensitive. You could write **onclick**, **ONCLICK**, or **OnClIcK** and it would work. But the convention is **onClick**, so we'll stick with that.

- A JavaScript statement (or more than one), enclosed in quotes, follows. When the user clicks the link, it executes.

One more thing to notice: **onClick="alert('Hi');"** The message inside the parentheses is surrounded by single quotes, not the double quotes we've been using for an *alert* string. In JavaScript code, you aren't allowed to nest double quotes within double quotes or single quotes within single quotes. Since the entire JavaScript statement is enclosed in double quotes, you have to enclose the *alert* message in single quotes.

But there's a problem with the markup above. **<a href="#"** tells the browser to reload the page. This means that if the user has scrolled

down to the link, the click, in addition to running the JavaScript code, will scroll the page back to the top—an action you don't normally want. I've included this flawed approach, using **<a href="#"**, because you'll run into it here and there in other people's work, but you'll probably prefer this approach:

```
<a href="JavaScript:void(0)" onClick="alert('Hi');">Click</a>
```

Now you've got exactly what you want. Nothing at all happens except for the JavaScript that executes.

In the example above, the click executes only a single JavaScript statement. But there is no limit to the number of JavaScript statements that you can enclose in the quotation marks. No limit, that is, except for common sense. As you'll see, there are better ways to trigger JavaScript than packing multiple statements into an inline *onClick* event. But let me show you the principle, with this example. When the user clicks, a first statement assigns 'hi' to a variable and a second statement displays an alert specifying the variable as the message.

```
<a href="JavaScript:void(0)" onClick="var greet='hi';
alert(greet);">Click</a>
```

As I've said, coding professionals frown on inline JavaScript. But if you do use this approach, it's more craftsmanlike to call a function. Here's a function.

```
1 function popup(message) {
2    alert(message);
3 }
```

This is the event-handler that calls the function.

```
<a href="JavaScript:void(0)" onClick="popup('Hi');">Click</a>
```

When the user clicks the link, the event-handler calls the function, passing the argument 'Hi' to it. The function displays an alert saying 'Hi'.

Find the interactive coding exercises for this chapter at http://www.ASmarterWayToLearn.com/js/45.html

46
Events: button

In the last chapter you learned how to repurpose a link to make it trigger an event when it's clicked, instead of loading a new page. You learned to do it with inline event-handling, not the best way, but the easiest to learn. Later in the book, you'll learn the approach that's preferred by most professionals—the scripting approach.

But even if you're using the inline method, when you want to give the user something to click, a more professional approach, usually, is to use a button rather than a link.

Suppose that when the user clicks a button, an alert displays saying, "Hello world!"

Here's the code.

```
<input type="button" value="Click" onClick="alert('Hello world!');">
```

The event handler is the same, whether you're coding a link or a button: `onClick="alert('Hello world!');"`

But the beginning of the code is different: `<input type="button" value="Click"`

Some pros would argue that the button code should be enclosed in form tags, but it's not absolutely necessary. And anyway, since we're already violating best practices by using inline event handlers, why not scandalize the pros with multiple violations? (You'll learn more respectable alternatives to inline event handlers later in the book.)

As an HTML coder you know that you can use an image as a hot link. The markup would look something like this.

```
<a href="summary-page.html"><img src="button-sum-pg.png"></a>
```

You can also use an image to trigger an event. Let's say that when the user clicks an image, an alert pops up. This is the code. Note that the code for the inline event handler is the same as before.

```
<img src="button-greet.png" onClick="alert('Hello world!');">
```

Or, if you want to be more professional about it, you could have the event trigger a function.

```
<img src="button-greet.png" onClick="greetTheUser();">
```

Find the interactive coding exercises for this chapter at http://www.ASmarterWayToLearn.com/js/46.html

47
Events: mouse

You've learned how to make things happen when the user clicks a link, a button, or an image, by using inline event-handling. Inline event handling isn't the best approach, but the easiest to learn. Later in the book, you'll learn the approach that's preferred by most professionals—the scripting approach.

But whether you're using the inline method or the preferred scripting method, the *onClick* event is only one of many kinds of events that your code can respond to. In this chapter, you'll learn how to make things happen when the user mouses over something on the page, and also when the user mouses away from it.

Suppose your page initially displays a "before" picture of a model. When the user mouses over the picture, it is replaced by an "after" picture. You might prefer to do this with CSS, but since this is a JavaScript book, I'll show you how to do it with an event handler.

This is the markup that replaces the *before* picture with the *after* picture.

```
<img src="before-pic.jpg" onMouseover="src='after-pic.jpg'">
```

It begins as a plain vanilla image tag: **<img src="before-pic.jpg"**

Then comes the event-handling keyword. The keyword is in camelCase—optional but widely used: **onMouseover**

An equal sign follows the keyword **onMouseover**, just as it does with **onClick**. Then comes the response to the event, which is in quotes: **"src='after-pic.jpg'">**

You may be surprised that the response to the event isn't written in JavaScript. It's HTML markup.

Note: The image source must be enclosed in single quotes, because of those double quotes that enclose the whole phrase.

You can use *onMouseover* event handling with other HTML elements, too. Here's a bit of inline code that displays an alert when a heading is moused over.

```
<h1 onMouseover="alert('Be sure to get your shopping done
today.');">World Ends Tomorrow</h1>
```

When the user mouses over the head, an alert displays.

In the example above, you might prefer to call a function that displays the alert rather than code the alert inline.

Here's a JavaScript alternative to the preferred CSS color-change on hover.

```
<a href="index.html" onMouseover="this.style.color =
'green';">Home Page</a>
```

When the user mouses over the link, it turns green.

At this point don't be concerned about the overall idea behind **this.style.color** in the example. For now, just memorize the sequence so you can repeat it in the exercises.

In the next example, the paragraph expands to include more information when the user hovers over it.

```
<p id="loris" onMouseover="expand();">Slow Loris: Mouse
over for more info</p>
```

At this point don't worry now about how the function **expand** grows the paragraph. You'll learn about that later.

In the example we started with, the model's before-and-after pictures, the *onMouseover* event handler replaces the "before" picture with the "after" picture when the user mouses over the image. Normally, you'd want the image to revert to the original when the user mouses away from the picture. So you'd combine the *onMouseover* event handler with the *onMouseout* event handler.

```
<img src="before-pic.jpg" onMouseover="src='after-pic.jpg'"

onMouseout="src='before-pic.jpg'">
```

Find the interactive coding exercises for this chapter at http://www.ASmarterWayToLearn.com/js/47.html

48
Events: fields

Let's say you have a text field for the user's email address. When the user clicks in the field to type her entry, the field turns yellow.

This is the markup that makes it happen.

```
Email:<br>
<input type="text" size="30"
onFocus="this.style.backgroundColor = 'yellow';">
```

Once again, I'm showing you the not-recommended inline way to handle an event, using it as a stepping stone for learning more professional event-handling later in the book. Again, I'm not explaining **this.style.backgroundColor**. Just memorize the sequence to use in the exercises.

The keyword here is **onFocus**. It tells JavaScript to do something when the user clicks in the field.

The syntax is the same as for other event handlers that you've already learned to code: a keyword, followed by an equal sign, followed by JavaScript or HTML in quotes.

After the user enters her email address—or not—and clicks outside the field or presses the tab key to move to another field—that is, when this field no longer has the focus—you want it to revert to a white background. You do this with the **onBlur** keyword, which is the opposite of **onFocus**.

This markup handles both the *onFocus* and the *onBlur* events.

```
Email:<br>
<input type="text" size="30"
onFocus="this.style.backgroundColor = 'yellow';"
onBlur="this.style.backgroundColor = 'white';">
```

When the user clicks into the field, it turns yellow. When she clicks out of the field, it reverts to white.

A slightly more professional approach would be to call functions that accomplish the same things.

```
Email:<br>
<input type="text" size="30" onFocus="makeFieldYellow();"
onBlur="makeFieldWhite();">
```

Find the interactive coding exercises for this chapter at http://www.ASmarterWayToLearn.com/js/48.html

49
Reading field values

Suppose you've included an email field in a form, and you've made it a required field. The form has a **submit** button that the user clicks to submit the information that he's entered in the form.

This is the markup that creates the form. I've simplified it, omitting any form action and other attributes, including linebreaks, that don't bear on what you're learning here.

```
<form>
  Email:
  <input type="text">
  <input type="submit" value="Submit">
</form>
```

So now in our stripped-down form markup, we've got these three elements:

1. The text "Email"

2. The text field for the user's email address

3. The **submit** button

I'm going to give the email field an id.

```
<form>
  Email:
  <input type="text" id="email">
  <input type="submit" value="Submit">
</form>
```

I'm going to add an event-handler, using the keyword **onSubmit**.

```
<form onSubmit="checkAddress('email');">
  Email:
  <input type="text" id="email">
  <input type="submit" value="Submit">
</form>
```

Now, when the user clicks the **submit** button, the function **checkAddress** executes. Note that, even though the action is a click on the **submit** button, the *onSubmit* event handler is in the form tag, not in the **submit** button tag.

When the form is submitted, the function **checkAddress** checks if the user has entered anything in the email field. If not, the function displays an alert reminding the user that the email address is required.

In order to do this, the function needs a way to read what's in the email field. This is where the id that I added to the field comes in. Here's the code for the function.

```
1 function checkAddress(fieldId) {
2   if (document.getElementById(fieldId).value === "") {
3     alert("Email address required.");
4   }
5 }
```

If there's no value in the email field, an alert displays telling the user that an email address is required.

This is the sequence you need to memorize:

1. The keyword **document**, followed by...

2. a dot, followed by...

3. the keyword **getElementById**, followed by...

4. the parameter, in parentheses, received from the calling code, **fieldId**, followed by...

5. another dot, followed by...

6. the keyword **value**

getElementById must be in camelCase. If you do what comes naturally and write **getElementByID**, with a cap "D," it won't work.

Some coders prefer to put the value found in the field into a variable:

```
1 function checkAddress(fieldId) {
2   var val = document.getElementById(fieldId).value;
3   if (val === "") {
4     alert("Email address required.");
5   }
6 }
```

Find the interactive coding exercises for this chapter at http://www.ASmarterWayToLearn.com/js/49.html

50
Setting field values

The user has entered her ZIP code in a form field. You want to save her the trouble of entering the city and state. So when she clicks out of the field, you fill in the city field for her.

Let me show you how to do that. To keep things simple, we'll pretend there are only three ZIP codes in the U.S. We'll also pretend that the user will infallibly enter one of these codes. We won't check for errors. And for this example, the JavaScript code will fill in only the city field, not the state. Here's the relevant markup for the form. (I'm omitting a form action, a **submit** button, and everything else that's not relevant to this chapter.)

```
<form>
  ZIP:<br>
  <input type="text" id="zip" onBlur="fillCity();"><br>
  City:<br>
  <input type="text" id="city">
</form>
```

When the user clicks out of the ZIP field, the *onBlur* event triggers the **fillCity** function. This is the code.

```
1   function fillCity() {
2     var cityName;
3     var zipEntered = document.getElementById("zip").value;
4     switch (zipEntered) {
5     case "60608" :
6       cityName = "Chicago";
7       break;
8     case "68114" :
9       cityName = "Omaha";
10      break;
11    case "53212" :
12      cityName = "Milwaukee";
13    }
14    document.getElementById("city").value = cityName;
15  }
```

This example shows that you can not only read a value in a field with `document.getElementById`..., but can also "write" a value into a field.

In this case, the function assigns the value found in the ZIP field to a variable. Then, using a *switch* statement, it matches the ZIP to a city name and assigns that name to a second variable. Then, using the variable, it places the city name in the city field.

Find the interactive coding exercises for this chapter at http://www.ASmarterWayToLearn.com/js/50.html

51
Reading and setting paragraph text

Your webpage initially displays a picture of a little mammal known as the slow loris, along with a single sentence:

> Slow lorises are a group of several species of strepsirrhine primates which make up the genus Nycticebus. Click for more.

When the user clicks the link, the paragraph expands:

> Slow lorises are a group of several species of strepsirrhine primates which make up the genus Nycticebus. They have a round head, narrow snout, large eyes, and a variety of distinctive coloration patterns that are species-dependent.

This is the markup.

```
<p id="slowLoris">
Slow lorises are a group of several species of
strepsirrhine primates which make up the genus
Nycticebus.<a href="javascript:void(0);"
onClick="expandLoris();">Click for more.</a>
</p>
```

An id is assigned to the paragraph, which will be used by the function. When the user clicks the link, a function, **expandLoris**, is called.

This is the function.

```
1 function expandLoris() {
2   var expandedParagraph = "Slow lorises are a group of
several species of trepsirrhine primates which make up the
genus Nycticebus. They have a round head, narrow snout,
large eyes, and a variety of distinctive coloration
patterns that are species-dependent.";
3   document.getElementById("slowLoris").innerHTML =
expandedParagraph;
4 }
```

Line 2 assigns the long version of the text to a variable. Then, identifying the paragraph by its id, line 3 replaces the original content, the **innerHTML**, with the text stored in the variable.

Almost anything, including HTML tags, can be inserted into the web page this way. For example, you could make this list appear on the page within, say, a div with the id "lorisList".

1. Slow loris

2. Fast loris

3. Just-right loris

This is the function that loads the list markup into the div, which has been given an id of "lorisList".

```
1 function placeAList() {
2   var listToPlace = "<ol><li>Slow loris</li><li>Fast
loris</li><li>Just-right loris</li></ol>";
3   document.getElementById("lorisList").innerHTML =
listToPlace;
4 }
```

Line 2 assigns all the HTML for the list to a variable. Line 3 places the HTML into the div that has been assigned the id "lorisList".

You can use **document.getElementById(element id).innerHTML** to read as well as "write" the contents of an element. For example, this function assigns whatever is in the paragraph, div, or other element with the id "content" to the variable **whatsThere**.

```
1 function peekAtContent() {
2   var whatsThere =
document.getElementById("content").innerHTML;
3 }
```

Line 2 reads all the HTML within the element with an id of "content" and assigns it to the variable **whatsThere**. If the element is a paragraph whose content is "Hello, Sailor!" the variable **whatsThere** captures "Hello, Sailor!"

Find the interactive coding exercises for this chapter at http://www.ASmarterWayToLearn.com/js/51.html

52
Manipulating images and text

Your webpage displays a picture of a blobfish. The blobfish is a fascinating animal, but it's so ugly, some of your users go "Yuck." So you give them the option of making it disappear. When they click the image, it vanishes.

You begin by giving the image an id.

```
<img src="blobfish.jpg" id="ugly"...
```

Then you add an event handler.

```
<img src="blobfish.jpg" id="ugly" onClick="makeInvisible();">
```

You have a CSS class for invisibility.

```
.hidden {display:none;}
```

The function called by the event handler gives the image a class of "hidden," so it disappears.

```
1 function makeInvisible() {
2 document.getElementById("ugly").className = "hidden";
3 }
```

When the function is called, it assigns the "hidden" class to the element with the id "ugly." The image disappears.

Some things to keep in mind:

- This is just a variation on things you've already learned, **document.getElementById(theElementId).value** (for form fields) and **document.getElementById(theElementId).innerHTML** (for paragraphs, divs, and other HTML elements).

- It's **className**, in camelCase, not **class**.

- Assigning a class to an element this way replaces any classes that the element has been assigned in the static markup.

If you want to add a class to an element, preserving its existing classes, you can do it. For example, suppose you have a paragraph with a class that styles it in Verdana, size 1 em. When the user mouses over it, you want to double its size to 2 em. But you don't want to lose the Verdana styling of its original class. Rather than replace the class that styles it in Verdana, you want to retain that class and add the class that enlarges the font. Let's say the element has the id "p1". This is the function.

```
1 function makeBig() {
2   document.getElementById("p1").className += " big";
3 }
```

Compared with the code that replaces all the existing classes with a new one, this code has two small differences.

- It's **+=** instead of just **=**.

- A space before the class name is required.

Find the interactive coding exercises for this chapter at http://www.ASmarterWayToLearn.com/js/52.html

53
Swapping images

In Chapter 47 you learned how to replace one image with another when the user mouses over the image. When the page first displays, a "before" picture is what the user sees. When the user mouses over the picture, it is replaced by an "after" picture.

You learned how to do this by coding an inline event handler that looks like this.

```
<img src="before-pic.jpg" onMouseover="src='after-pic.jpg'">
```

Another way to do it is to call a function that makes the swap. This is the markup:

```
<img src="before-pic.jpg" id="before"
onMouseover="swapPic();">
```

This is the function code.

```
1 function swapPic() {
2     document.getElementById("before").src = "after-pic.jpg";
3 }
```

But why not make the function a general-purpose routine that can swap any image for any other image? In order for this to work, the markup has to pass both the id and the name of the replacement image to the function as arguments.

```
<img src="before-pic.jpg" id="before"
onMouseover="swapPic(id,'after-pic.jpg');">
```

The function accepts these arguments as its parameters and uses them to swap the images.

```
1 function swapPic(eId, newPic) {
2     document.getElementById(eId).src = newPic;
3 }
```

Find the interactive coding exercises for this chapter at http://www.ASmarterWayToLearn.com/js/53.html

54
Swapping images and setting classes

You've been learning how to read the properties of HTML elements, and also how to change those properties using various statements that incorporate the magic words **document.getElementById**.... For example, the following function removes the original image, with the id of "before," and replaces it with a second image, "after-pic.jpg."

```
1 function swapPic() {
2   document.getElementById("before").src = "after-pic.jpg";
3 }
```

A more common way to code the function is to break it into two steps, first assigning **document.getElementById("before")** to a variable. Then you combine that variable with **.src**. Let's call it the verbose approach.

```
1 function swapPic() {
2   var pic = document.getElementById("before");
3   pic.src = "after-pic.jpg";
4 }
```

Here's a function that uses the verbose approach to find out the address of a link that has the id "link1".

```
1 function getAddress() {
2   var link = document.getElementById("link1");
3   var address = link.href;
4 }
```

The function probes the **href** property of the link tag. For example, if **href** equals "http://wikipedia.org" that address winds up in the variable **address**.

This function changes the formatting of a form that has the id "f12" by changing its class.

```
1 function enlargeForm() {
2   var frm = document.getElementById("f12");
3   frm.className = "jumbo";
4 }
```

Find the interactive coding exercises for this chapter at
http://www.ASmarterWayToLearn.com/js/54.html

55
Setting styles

In Chapter 52 you learned how to add a css class to any element to change its styling. For example, this function adds the class "big" to an element. If, for example, the new class, "big," specifies a larger font size for the element than it has originally, the result is that the text inside the element gets bigger.

```
1 function makeBig() {
2   document.getElementById("p1").className += " big";
3 }
```

There's another way to specify style properties.

```
1 function makeBig() {
2   document.getElementById("p1").style.fontSize = "2em";
3 }
```

Like the first example, the function changes the default font size of an element with the id "p1". But, unlike the first example, it doesn't remove any other styles assigned to the element, whether those styles are specified in css or inline.

Example: If the heading, paragraph, or div has an initial size of 1em, the function doubles the size of its contents. If the element has an initial style of bold Georgia italic with 12-pixel borders, all of this formatting is preserved. Only the size changes.

This statement left-floats an image.

```
document.getElementById("pic99").style.cssFloat = "left";
```

This statement makes an element invisible.

```
document.getElementById("div9").style.visibility = "hidden";
```

This statement gives an element left and right margins of 10 pix.

```
document.getElementById("mainPic").style.margin = "0 10px 0
10px";
```

You can set many style properties this way. Sometimes the terms for property specs aren't obvious, so it's best to check the language rules—is it "float" or "cssFloat"?—rather than guessing.

As usual, you can read properties as well as set them. However, the rules aren't straightforward. If you write...

```
var m = document.getElementById("mainPic").style.margin;
```

...it'll tell you only the margins specified inline, if any. If margins are specified in css, you won't get them. The following statement gives you all the style properties, specified in both css and inline, but it has a limitation. Versions of Internet Explorer before Version 9 don't support it.

```
var m = window.getComputedStyle("mainPic").margin;
```

Find the interactive coding exercises for this chapter at http://www.ASmarterWayToLearn.com/js/55.html

56
Target all elements by tag name

Suppose you want to give your users the option of doubling the size of the text in all the paragraphs of the document. To accomplish this, you could give each paragraph an id. When the user clicks the **Double Text Size** button, a function would cycle through all the paragraph ids and make the change. The function could upsize the font either by assigning a new class to each paragraph, with the class specifying a larger font size, or it could assign the new style property directly, like this:

```
getElementById(the id).style.fontSize = "2em";
```

An easier way to accomplish the same thing is to have the function say, "Find all the paragraphs in the document and increase their size." This statement finds all the paragraphs and assigns them to a variable:

```
var par = document.getElementsByTagName("p");
```

The variable, **par**, now holds an array-like collection of all the paragraphs in the document. Suppose, to keep things simple, that the body of the document comprises just three paragraphs.

```
<p>This bed is too small.</p>
<p>This bed is too big.</p>
<p>This bed is just right.</p>
```

par[0] is the first paragraph. **par[1]** is the second paragraph. **par[2]** is the third paragraph. **par.length** is 3, the number of items in the collection.

If you write...

```
var textInMiddleParagraph = par[1].innerHTML;
```

...the variable **textInMiddleParagraph** is assigned "This bed is too big."

If you write...

```
par[1].innerHTML = "This SUV is too big.";
```

...the paragraph text changes to "This SUV is too big."

Here's a loop that assigns a font family to all the paragraphs.

```
1 for (var i = 0; i < par.length; i++) {
2    par[i].style.fontFamily = "Verdana, Geneva, sans-
serif";
3 }
```

This statement makes a collection of all the images in the document and assigns it to the variable **pics**.

```
var pics = document.getElementsByTagName("img");
```

This statement makes a collection of all the divs in the document and assigns it to the variable **divs**.

```
var divs = document.getElementsByTagName("div");
```

This statement makes a collection of all the unordered lists in the document and assigns it to the variable **ulists**.

```
var ulists = document.getElementsByTagName("ul");
```

Find the interactive coding exercises for this chapter at http://www.ASmarterWayToLearn.com/js/56.html

57
Target some elements by tag name

In the last chapter you learned how to make an array-like collection of all the elements in a document that have a particular tag name. For example, this statement makes a collection of all the paragraphs in the document and assigns the collection to the variable **pars**.

```
var pars = document.getElementsByTagName("p");
```

You also learned to read or set the properties of any of the elements in a collection of elements by using array-like notation—a number in square brackets. For example, this statement "reads" the contents of the second element in the collection **pars** and assigns the string to the variable **textInMiddleParagraph**.

```
var textInMiddleParagraph = pars[1].innerHTML;
```

But suppose you don't want a collection of all the paragraphs in the document. Suppose you want just a collection of all the paragraphs within a particular div. No problem. Let's say the id of the div is "rules". Here's the code.

```
1 var e = document.getElementById("rules");
2 var paragraphs = e.getElementsByTagName("p");
Line 1 assigns the div with the id "rules" to the variable
e.
```

Line 2 makes a collection of all the paragraphs in the div and assigns the collection to the variable **paragraphs**.

Once the id of the target div has been assigned to a variable, for example **e**, you can assemble a collection of all the paragraphs within that div. Instead of writing...

```
document.getElementsByTagName("p");
```

...which would make a collection of all the paragraphs in the document, you write...

```
e.getElementsByTagName("p");
```

...which makes a collection of all the paragraphs in the div.

Suppose you have a table with a white background. When the user clicks a button, the cells turn pink. Here's the code.

```
1 var t = document.getElementById("table9");
2 var cells = t.getElementsByTagName("td");
3 for (var i = 0; i < cells.length; i++) {
4   cells[i].style.backgroundColor = "pink";
5 }
```

Here's the line-by-line breakdown.

1. Targets the table by its id

2. Assembles a collection of all the elements in the table with a **td** tag

3-5. Loops through all of them to change their background color

Find the interactive coding exercises for this chapter at http://www.ASmarterWayToLearn.com/js/57.html

58
The DOM

In previous chapters you learned two different ways to target components of your web page so you could read or set them. You learned to **getElementById**, and you learned to **getElementsByTagName**. These are often the best methods for targeting things, but they have limitations. The first, **getElementById**, gives you access only to those components that have been assigned an id. The second, **getElementsByTagName**, is good for wholesale changes, but is a bit cumbersome for fine surgical work. Both approaches can change things on your web page, but neither is able to deal with all the things on the page, to create new things, to move existing things, or to delete them.

Fortunately, both of these approaches are only two of many methods for working with the *Document Object Model,* the *DOM.* The DOM is an organization chart, created automatically by the browser when your web page loads, for the whole web page. All the things on your web page—the tags, the text blocks, the images, the links, the tables, the style attributes, and more—have spots on this organization chart. This means that your JavaScript code can get its hands on anything on your web page, anything at all, just by saying where that thing is on the chart. What's more, your JavaScript can add things, move things, or delete things by manipulating the chart. If you wanted to (you wouldn't), you could almost create an entire web page from scratch using JavaScript's DOM methods.

Here's a simplified web page. I've indented the different levels in the hierarchy. The three top levels of the DOM are always the same for a standard web page. The document is the first level. Under the document is the second level, the html. And under the html are the co-equal third levels, the head and the body. Under each of these are more levels.

```
1st level: document
2nd level:    <html>
3rd level:     <head>
4th level:      <title>
5th level:        Simple document
                </title>
              </head>
3rd level     <body>
4th level       <p>
5th level         There's not much to this.
                </p>
              </body>
            </html>
```

Here's the same thing, shown as an organization chart. Note that this is an idealized chart, cleaned of junk artifacts that most browsers insert in the DOM. I'll show you how to clean out these artifacts in later chapters.

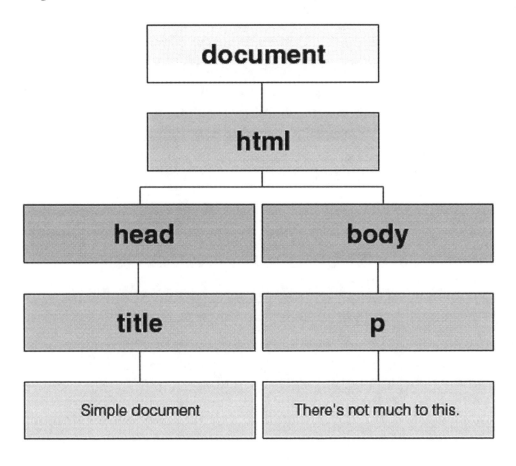

As you can see, every single thing on the web page is included, even the title text and the paragraph text. Let's make it a little more complicated by adding a div and a second paragraph. Here it is in HTML form.

```
1st level: document
2nd level:    <html>
3rd level:      <head>
4th level:        <title>
5th level:          Simple document
                  </title>
              </head>
3rd level     <body>
4th level       <div>
5th level        <p>
6th level           There's not much to this.
                 </p>
5th level        <p>
6th level           Nor to this.
                 </p>
              </div>
            </body>
          </html>
```

And in an organization chart (minus any junk artifacts)...

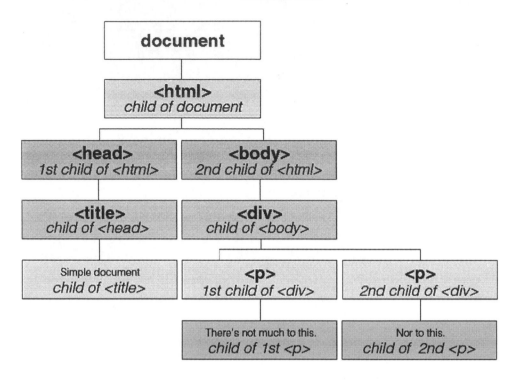

In a company organization chart, each box represents a person. In the DOM organization chart, each box represents a *node*. The HTML page represented above, in its cleaned-up DOM form, has 11 nodes: the document node, the html node, the head and body nodes, the title node, the div node, two paragraph nodes, and three text nodes, one for the title and one for each of the two paragraphs.

In this particular chart, there are three types of nodes: document, element, and text. The document node is the top level. Element nodes are **<html>**, **<head>**, **<body>**, **<title>**, **<div>**, and **<p>**. Text nodes are the strings that comprise the title and the two paragraphs.

Find the interactive coding exercises for this chapter at http://www.ASmarterWayToLearn.com/js/58.html

59
The DOM: Parents and children

Can you name the second child of the 44th President of the United States? That would be Sasha. How about the parent (male) of the 43rd President? That's right. It's George.

Welcome to the most fundamental way of designating nodes of the Document Object Model (DOM). You can designate any node of the DOM by saying the node is the *x*th child of a particular parent. You can also designate a node by saying it's the parent of any child.

Take a look at the simplified html document from the last chapter.

```
1st level: document
2nd level:    <html>
3rd level:      <head>
4th level:        <title>
5th level:          Simple document
                 </title>
              </head>
3rd level        <body>
4th level          <div>
5th level            <p>
6th level              There's not much to this.
                     </p>
5th level            <p>
6th level              Nor to this.
                     </p>
                  </div>
               </body>
            </html>
```

Except for the document node, each node is enclosed within another node. The **<head>** and **<body>** nodes are enclosed within the **<html>** node. The **<div>** node is enclosed within the **<body>** node. Two **<p>** nodes are enclosed within the **<div>** node. And a text node is enclosed within each of the **<p>** nodes.

When a node is enclosed within another node, we say that the enclosed node is a *child* of the node that encloses it. So, for example, the **<div>** node is a child of the **<body>** node. Conversely, the **<body>**

node is the *parent* of the **<div>** node. Here's the organization chart from the last chapter, again cleaned of junk artifacts, showing all the parents and their children.

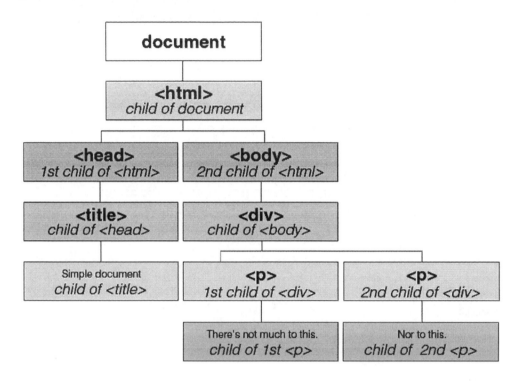

As you can see, **<html>** is the child of the document...**<head>** and **<body>** are the children of **<html>**...**<div>** is the child of **<body>**...two **<p>**'s are the children of **<div>**...each text node is the child of a **<p>**. Conversely, the document is the parent of **<html>**, **<html>** is the parent of **<head>** and **<body>**, **<head>** is the parent of **<title>**, **<title>** is the parent of a text node, and so on. Nodes with the same parent are known as *siblings*. So, **<head>** and **<body>** are siblings because **<html>** is the parent of both. The two **<p>**'s are siblings because **<div>** is the parent of both.

Starting at the bottom of the chart, the text "Nor to this." is a child of **<p>**, which is a child of **<div>**, which is a child of **<body>**, which is a child of **<html>**, which is a child of the document.

Now look at this markup.

```
<p>This is <em>important</em>!</p>
```

If you made a chart for this paragraph, you might think that all the text is a child of the **<p>** node. But remember, every node that is enclosed by another node is the child of the node that encloses it. Since the text node "important" is enclosed by the element node **<em>**, this particular text node is the child of **<em>**, not **<p>**. The text nodes "This is " and "!" as well as the element node **<em>** are siblings, because they're all enclosed by **<p>**. They're all children of **<p>**.

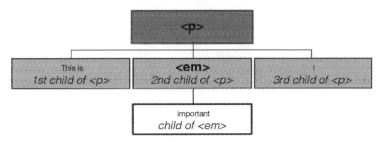

Find the interactive coding exercises for this chapter at http://www.ASmarterWayToLearn.com/js/59.html

60
The DOM:
Finding children

As you learned in the last chapter, the Document Object Model (DOM) is a hierarchy of parents and children. Everything on the web page, excluding the document itself, is a child of something else. So now let's talk about how your JavaScript code can make use of this hierarchy of parents and children to read or change virtually anything on a web page.

Let's begin with the methods you've already learned for targeting things on the web page. You'll recall from earlier chapters that you can target an element by specifying its id, if it has one.

```
var eField = document.getElementById("email");
```

The statement above targets the element with the id of "email"

You also learned how to make an array-like collection of all the elements of a particular kind within the document...

```
var eField = document.getElementsByTagName("p");
```

Having made a collection of paragraphs, you can target any paragraph within the collection so that you can, for example, read its contents.

```
var contents = p[2].innerHTML;
```

The statement above assigns the text string contained within the third paragraph of the document to the variable **contents**.

An alternative to listing all the elements of a certain kind in the document is to narrow the focus below the document level, for example to a div, and then make a collection within that div.

```
1 var d = document.getElementById("div3");
2 var p = d.getElementsByTagName("p");
3 var contents = p[2].innerHTML;
```

In the example above, you can generate a collection not of all the paragraph elements in the document, but only those paragraph elements within the div that has an id of "div3". Then you target one of those paragraphs.

Now consider this markup.

```
<body>
  <div id="cal">
    <p>Southern Cal is sunny.</p>
    <p>Northern Cal is rainy.</p>
    <p>Eastern Cal is desert.</p>
  </div>
  <div id="ny">
    <p>Urban NY is crowded.</p>
    <p>Rural NY is sparse.</p>
  </div>
</body>
```

If you wanted to read the contents of the last paragraph in the markup, you could write...

```
1 var p = document.getElementsByTagName("p");
2 var contents = p[4].innerHTML;
```

Line 1 makes a collection of all the **<p>**s in the document and assigns the collection to the variable **p**. Line 2 "reads" the text contained in the 5th paragraph of the document.

Another approach: You could target the same paragraph by narrowing the collection of elements to those that are just in the second div.

```
1 var div = document.getElementById("ny");
2 var p = div.getElementsByTagName("p");
3 var contents = p[1].innerHTML;
```

Here's the breakdown:

1. Assigns the div with the id "ny" to the variable **div**

2. Makes a collection of all the **<p>**s in the div and assigns the collection to the variable **p**

3. "Reads" the text contained in the 2nd paragraph of the div and assigns it to the variable **contents**

Now I'll show you a new way to target the paragraph, by using the DOM organization chart.

```
1 var p =
document.childNodes[0].childNodes[1].childNodes[1].childNodes[1];
2 var contents = p.innerHTML;
```

I'll highlight each child level and tell you what it points to.

   document.childNodes[0].childNodes[1].childNodes[1].childNodes[1]; is the first child of the document, **<html>**
   document.childNodes[0].childNodes[1].childNodes[1].childNodes[1]; is the second child of **<html>**, **<body>**
   document.childNodes[0].childNodes[1].childNodes[1].childNodes[1]; is the second child of **<body>**, **<div>** with the id "ny"
   document.childNodes[0].childNodes[1].childNodes[1].childNodes[1]; is the second child of **<div>** with the id "ny", the second **<p>** within the div

Note: The code above assumes the browser hasn't included any junk artifacts in the DOM. I'll discuss these in the next chapter.

As we work our way down the organization chart, each parent is followed by a dot, which is followed by the keyword **childNodes**, which is followed by a number in brackets, as in array notation. As in array notation, the first child is number 0.

Here's the markup again. The key players in the code above are highlighted.

```
<body>
  <div id="cal">
    <p>Southern Cal is sunny.</p>
    <p>Northern Cal is rainy.</p>
    <p>Eastern Cal is desert.</p>
  </div>
  <div id="ny">
    <p>Urban NY is crowded.</p>
    <p>Rural NY is sparse.</p>
  </div>
</body>
```

In the example above, I showed you how to work your way down to the targeted node starting at the document level. But in practice, you'd normally start at a lower level. For example, you could start with the second div, specifying its id. Then you'd target one of its children.

```
1 var d = document.getElementById("ny");
2 var p = d.childNodes[1];
3 var contents = p.innerHTML;
```

Find the interactive coding exercises for this chapter at http://www.ASmarterWayToLearn.com/js/60.html

61
The DOM: Junk artifacts and nodeType

The diagram below is valid for only a couple of browsers. Most browsers interpret the whitespace that's created by some carriage returns, tabs, and spaces as text nodes. When you look at the markup, you see 3 text nodes:

```
1st level: document
2nd level:    <html>
3rd level:      <head>
4th level:        <title>
5th level:          Simple document
                  </title>
                </head>
3rd level       <body>
4th level         <div>
5th level           <p>
6th level             There's not much to this.
                    </p>
5th level           <p>
6th level             Nor to this.
                    </p>
                  </div>
                </body>
              </html>
```

Firefox sees this markup with 8 additional text nodes that are nothing but whitespace created by indenting—junk artifacts.

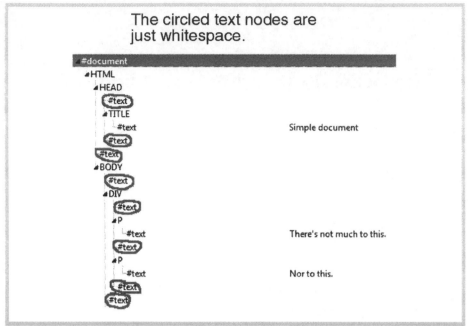

The circled text nodes are just whitespace.

These extra text nodes create noise that makes it hard for your DOM-reading code to find the signal. In one browser, the first child of the body node might be a div. In another browser, the first child of the body might be an empty text node.

There are a number of solutions. As one approach, the Mozilla Developer Network suggests a workaround that's almost comically desperate but does solve the problem without any extra effort from JavaScript. You format the markup like this.

```
<html
><head
><title
>Simple document
</title
></head
><body
><div
><p
>There's not much to this.
</p
><p
>Nor to this.
</p
></div
></body
```

```
></html>
```

This markup takes advantage of the fact that any carriage returns, tabs, and spaces that are enclosed in the **<** and the **>** of a tag are ignored by the browser. To the browser, **< p >** is the same as **<p>**. And...

```
<
div
>
```

...is the same as **<div>**.

When whitespace is inside the brackets, the browser doesn't count it as a text node. So if you "hide" all carriage returns, tabs, and spaces inside the brackets as the code above does, there's no junk in the DOM. Any noise that would keep your JavaScript from reading the signal is removed.

You can also clean out junk in the DOM by using a *minifier* program like the one at http://www.willpeavy.com/minifier/ that removes carriage returns, tabs, and spaces that create junk. You will, of course, want to preserve the original, non-minified version of the file so you can revise the page in the future without going crazy. This is what minified code looks like:

```
<html><head><title>Simple
document</title></head><body><div><p>There's not much to
this.</p><p>Nor to this.</p></div></body></html>
```

Another approach is to format your HTML conventionally and let your JavaScript sniff out the junk nodes. JavaScript can check a node to see what type it is—element, text, comment, and so on. For example, this statement checks the node type of a targeted node and assigns it to the variable **nType**.

```
var nType = targetNode.nodeType;
```

In the statement above, JavaScript assigns a number representing the node type to the variable **nType**. If the node is an element like **<div>** or **<p>**, the number is 1. If it's a text node, the number is 3.

Suppose you want to replace the text content of the second paragraph in a particular div with the string "All his men." Here's the markup, with the text we're going to change highlighted.

```
<div id="humpty">
  <p>All the king's horses.</p>
  <p>All the dude's crew.</p>
  <p>All the town's orthopedists.</p>
</div>
```

This is the code.

```
1  var d = document.getElementById("humpty");
2  var pCounter = 0;
3  for (var i = 0; i < d.childNodes.length; i++) {
4    if (d.childNodes[i].nodeType === 1 ) {
5      pCounter++;
6    }
7    if (pCounter === 2) {
8      d.childNodes[i].innerHTML = "All his men.";
9      break;
10   }
11 }
```

Here's the breakdown:

1 Assigns the div to the variable **d**
2 Counts the number of paragraphs
3 Goes through the children of the div looking for the next element node, i.e. Type 1, which we assume is a paragraph
4-6 Adds 1 to the counter. We're looking for the second paragraph.
7-9 When the counter hits 2, we've reached the targeted paragraph.

If you know you might want your code to change the second paragraph, why not just assign it an id, and go straight to it, like this.

```
document.getElementById("p2").innerHTML = "All his men.";
```

You can see why the **getElementById** method is more popular with coders than tracing the DOM hierarchy. But there are some things you can't do without working your way through the parent-child relationships of the DOM, as you'll learn in subsequent chapters.

Find the interactive coding exercises for this chapter at http://www.ASmarterWayToLearn.com/js/61.html

62
The DOM: More ways to target elements

So far you've learned to use the DOM's parent-child hierarchy to target a child node of a parent node by specifying its order in an array-like collection of children—**childNodes[0], childNodes[1], childNodes[2],** and so on. But there are other ways to use the hierarchy for targeting. To begin with, instead of writing **childNodes[0]**, you can write **firstChild**. And instead of writing, for example, **childNodes[9]**, to target the 10th child in a 10-child collection of children, you can write **lastChild**.

```
var targetNode = parentNode.childNodes[0];
```

...is the same as...

```
var targetNode = parentNode.firstChild;
```

And if there are, for example, 3 child nodes...

```
var targetNode = parentNode.childNodes[2];
```

...is the same as...

```
var targetNode = parentNode.lastChild;
```

You can also work backwards, targeting the parent node of any child node. Let's say you have this markup. Using the DOM, how do you find the parent of the highlighted div?

```
<div id="div1">
  <div id="div2">
    <p>Chicago</p>
    <p>Kansas City</p>
    <p>St. Louis</p>
  </div>
</div>
```

You want to know the parent of the div with the id "div2". The following code assigns the parent of the "div2" div to the variable **pNode**.

```
1 var kidNode = document.getElementById("div2");

2 var pNode = kidNode.parentNode;
```

You can use **nextSibling** and **previousSibling** to target the next child and the previous child in the collection of an element's children. In the following code, the first statement targets a div with the id "div1". The second statement targets the next node that has the same parent as the "div1" id.

```
1 var firstEl = document.getElementById("div1");
2 secondEl = firstEl.nextSibling;
```

If there is no **nextSibling** or **previousSibling**, you get null. In the following code, the variable **nonexistentEl** has a value of null, because JavaScript finds that there is no previous node that has the same parent as **firstEl**.

```
1 var firstEl = document.getElementById("div1");
2 var nonexistentEl = firstEl.previousSibling;
```

Counting siblings can be tricky, because, as you know, some browsers treat whitespace created by HTML formatting as text nodes, even though they're empty and without significance.

In the HTML example above, with two divs and three paragraphs, you might think that the next sibling of the first paragraph is the second paragraph. But actually, in some browsers, the first paragraph's next sibling is an empty text node. The next sibling of that node is the second paragraph.

What this means is that in order to target a node with **nextSibling** or **previousSibling**, you have to either format your HTML markup defensively as I showed you in the last chapter, or else type-test each node to make sure it's the kind you're looking for, as I also showed you in the last chapter.

Once again, I'll say that you're often better off assigning an id to any node you might want to "read" or change. Then you can target the node more directly, using **document.getElementById**.

Find the interactive coding exercises for this chapter at http://www.ASmarterWayToLearn.com/js/62.html

63
The DOM: Getting a target's name

In a previous chapter you learned how to get a node's node type with a statement like this.

```
var nType = targetNode.nodeType;
```

In the example above, if the node is an element, the variable **nType** will be assigned the number 1. If the node is text, it'll be assigned the number 3.

You can get additional information about a node by using **nodeName**. In the following example, the node name of the target node is assigned to the variable **nName**.

```
1 var parent = document.getElementById("div1");
2 var target = parent.firstChild;
3 nName = target.nodeName;
```

Lines 1 and 2 target the first child of an element with the id "div1". Line 3 assigns the node name of the target to the variable **nName**.

In the example above, if the node is an element, the variable **nName** will be assigned a string, like P or DIV, that corresponds to the characters of the tag that are enclosed in the brackets. In HTML, the name is usually given in all-caps, even if the markup is in lowercase.

Tag	Node Name
\<p> or \<P>	P
\<div> or \<DIV>	DIV
\<span> or \<SPAN>	SPAN
\<img> or \<IMG>	IMG
\<a> or \<A>	A
\<em> or \<EM>	EM
\<table> or \<TABLE>	TABLE
\<li> or \<LI>	LI

On the other hand, if the node is a text node, the name of the node is always #text—in lower-case.

If it's a text node, you can find out its value—i.e. its content—this way.

```
1 var parent = document.getElementById("div1");
2 var target = parent.firstChild;
3 var nTextContent = target.nodeValue;
```

Lines 1 and 2 target the first child of an element with the id "div1". Line 3 assigns the node value to the variable **nTextContent**.

So if this is the markup, with the first child of the H2 element a node with the name "#text"...

```
<h2>Do <em>not</em> hit!</h2>
```

...the node value is "Do ".

An element node like P or IMG has a name but no value. If you try to assign an element node value to a variable, the variable will be assigned null.

```
<h2>Do <em>not</em> hit!</h2>
```

In the above example, <em> is an element, which means its value is null.

It's possible to confuse the node value of a text node with the **innerHTML property**. There are two differences.

- **innerHTML** is a property of the element node, <h2>, in the above example. The node value is a property of the text node itself, not the parent element.

- **innerHTML** includes all the descendants of the element, including any inner element nodes like <em> as well as text nodes. The node value includes only the characters that comprise the single text node.

In the following code, the **innerHTML** of the H2 element is highlighted.

```
<h2>Do <em>not</em> hit!</h2>
```

In the following code, the node value of the first child of the H2 element is highlighted.

```
<h2>Do <em>not</em> hit!</h2>
```

Since there are situations in which **nodeName** gets you, for example, a "p" instead of a "P" or an "href" instead of an "HREF," it's good practice to standardize the case when you're testing for names, like this.

```
if (targetNode.nodeName.toLowerCase() === "img") {
```

If the node name was originally upper-case, the code changes it to lower-case. If it was lower-case to begin with, no harm done.

If you're checking a node name to see if a node is a text node, converting to lower-case isn't necessary, because the name of a text node is always "#text", never "#TEXT".

Find the interactive coding exercises for this chapter at:
http://www.ASmarterWayToLearn.com/js/63.html

64
The DOM: Counting elements

In an earlier chapter you learned how to make an array-like collection of all the elements that share a particular tag name. For example, the following code makes a collection of all the **<li>** elements and assigns the collection to the variable **liElements**.

```
var liElements = getElementsByTagName("li");
```

Once you have the collection of elements, you can find out how many of them there are. In the following code, the number of **<li>** elements in the collection represented by **liElements** is assigned to the variable **howManyLi**.

```
var howManyLi = liElements.length;
```

Then you can, for example, cycle through the collection looking for <li> elements that have no text, and can enter some placeholder text.

```
1 for (var i = 0; i < howManyLi; i++) {
2   if (liElements[i].innerHTML === "") {
3     liElements[i].innerHTML = "coming soon";
4   }
5 }
```

I've walked you through this to introduce you to an analogous move you can make using the DOM hierarchy rather than tag names. You can make a collection of all the child nodes of a targeted node.

```
1 var parentNode = document.getElementById("d1");
2 var nodeList = parentNode.childNodes;
```

Line 1 assigns an element with the id "d1" to the variable **parentNode**. Line 2 assigns a collection of the child nodes of **parentNode** to **nodeList**.

You can get the number of items in the collection. The following statement assigns the number of items in the node collection to the variable **howManyKids**.

```
var howManyKids = nodeList.length;
```

Then you can target any item in the collection. The following code counts the number of images within the div.

```
1 var numberPics = 0;
2 for (var i = 0; i < howManyKids; i++) {
3   if (nodelist[i].nodeName.toLowerCase() === "img") {
4     numberPics++;
5   }
6 }
```

Here's the breakdown:

1 Declares the image-counter and sets it at 0

2 Loops through all the children of the div

3-5 If the node name, converted to lower-case, is "img", increments the image-counter

Find the interactive coding exercises for this chapter at http://www.ASmarterWayToLearn.com/js/64.html

65
The DOM: Attributes

Take a look at this bit of markup.

```
<a href="http://www.amazon.com">Shop</a>
```

You've learned that in the above markup the text node "Shop" is the first (and only) child of the element node <a>. But what is **href="http://www.amazon.com"**? It's definitely a node of the DOM, and you could say that it's subsidiary to <a>. But it's not a child of <a>. It's an *attribute* of <a>.

Whenever you see this form...

```
<element something="something in quotes">
```

...you're looking at an element with an attribute. The equal sign and the quotes are the tipoff. The word on the left side of the equal sign is the attribute name. The word on the right side of the equal sign is the attribute value. Here are more examples. The attribute values are highlighted.

```
<div id="p1">
<p class="special">
<img src="images/slow-loris.png">
<span style="font-size:24px;">
```

An element can have any number of attributes. In this tag, the element img has 4 attributes. I've highlighted their values.

```
<img src="dan.gif" alt="Dan" height="42" width="42">
```

You can find out whether an element has a particular attribute with **hasAttribute**.

```
1 var target = document.getElementById("p1");
2 var hasClass = target.hasAttribute("class");
```

Line 1 assigns the element to a variable, target. Line 2 checks to see if the element has an attribute called "class". If it does, the variable **hasClass** is assigned **true**. If not, it is assigned **false**.

You can read the value of an attribute with **getAttribute**.

```
1 var target = document.getElementById("div1");
2 var attVal = target.getAttribute("class");
```

Line 1 assigns the element to a variable, target. Line 2 reads the value of the attribute and assigns it to the variable **attVal**.

You can set the value of an attribute with **setAttribute**.

```
1 var target = document.getElementById("div1");
2 target.setAttribute("class", "special");
```

Line 1 assigns the element to a variable, **target**. Line 2 gives it an attribute "class" (the first specification inside the parentheses) with a value of "special" (the second specification inside the parentheses). In effect, the markup becomes:

```
<div id="div1" class="special">
```

Find the interactive coding exercises for this chapter at http://www.ASmarterWayToLearn.com/js/65.html

66
The DOM: Attribute names and values

In previous chapters you learned how to make a collection of elements that share the same tag name, with a statement like this...

```
var list = document.getElementsByTagName("p");
```

...and how to make a collection of all the children of an element, with a statement like this...

```
var list = document.getElementById("p1").childNodes;
```

Similarly, you can make a collection of all the attributes of an element, with a statement like this...

```
var list = document.getElementById("p1").attributes;
```

With the collection assigned to a variable, you can get the number of items in the collection...

```
var numOfItems = list.length;
```

Alternatively, you could compress these tasks into a single statement, without assigning the target to a variable first.

```
var numOfItems = document.getElementById("p1").attributes.length;
```

Using array-like notation, you can find out the name of any attribute in the collection. The following statement targets the third item in the collection of attributes and assigns its name to the variable **nName**.

```
var nName = list[2].nodeName;
```

For example, if the markup is...

```
<p id="p1" class="c1" onMouseover="chgColor();">
```

...the variable **nName** is assigned "onmouseover".

Note that the node name comes back not in the camelCase it was written in, but all lowercase: "onmouseover." Similarly, if your HTML says, "onClick," it'll come back "onclick." If the HTML says "onFocus," it'll come back "onfocus," and so on.

You can also get the value of the attribute...

```
var nValue = list[2].nodeValue;
```

In the example markup above, the variable **nValue** is assigned "chgColor();".

Find the interactive coding exercises for this chapter at http://www.ASmarterWayToLearn.com/js/66.html

67
The DOM: Adding nodes

Using the DOM hierarchy, you can add element, attribute, and text nodes anywhere in the head or body sections of a document. In this chapter you'll learn how to create a paragraph node, give it an attribute, and fill it with text content. In the next chapter, you'll learn how to insert the paragraph, along with its attributes and text content, into the page.

The first step is to create the paragraph node.

```
var nodeToAdd = document.createElement("p");
```

The example creates a paragraph element. To create a div element, you'd put "div" in the parentheses. To create an image element, you'd put "img" there. To create a link, you'd put "a" there. And so on.

Here's a statement that creates an image element.

```
var imgNodeToAdd = document.createElement("img");
```

In the last chapter, you learned how to add an attribute to an element that's already part of the web page, using **setAttribute**. You can do the same thing with an element that you've created but haven't yet placed in the document body.

```
nodeToAdd.setAttribute("class", "regular");
```

The code above gives the new paragraph element that you just created the class "regular". If you wanted to, you could add, using separate statements for each, more attributes to the paragraph element—for example, a span, a style, even an id.

If the element were an <img> element, you could add a border or an alt as an attribute. If it were an <a> element, you could add the web address.

This statement adds a border attribute to an image element.

```
imgNodeToAdd.setAttribute("border", "1");
```

The code above gives the image a 1-pixel border.

Remember, at this point, we're just creating nodes. The new attribute node has been connected to the new element node, but we haven't added the nodes to the page yet.

Getting back to the paragraph element, we've created it and added a class attribute to it. Now let's give it some text content. Again, we begin by creating the node we want.

```
var newTxt = document.createTextNode("Hello!");
```

The statement above creates a text node with the content "Hello!"
Next, we place the text into the paragraph element.

```
nodeToAdd.appendChild(newTxt);
```

The statement above adds the new text node, whose content is "Hello!", to the new paragraph node.

Now we have a new paragraph node with a class attribute and some text content. We're ready to insert it into the page.

Find the interactive coding exercises for this chapter at http://www.ASmarterWayToLearn.com/js/67.html

68
The DOM: Inserting nodes

In the last chapter you learned how to add text content to an element by first creating a text node and then appending the node to the element with **appendChild**. You can of course use the same method to append the paragraph element itself, filled with content or not, to a parent node, for example the body or a div. This set of statements targets a div (line 1), creates a new paragraph element (line 2), creates the text to go in it (line 3), places the text into the paragraph (line 4) and then appends the paragraph element along with its text content to the targeted div (line 5).

```
1 var parentDiv = document.getElementById("div1");
2 var newParagraph = document.createElement("p");
3 var t = document.createTextNode("Hello world!");
4 newParagraph.appendChild(t);
5 parentDiv.appendChild(newParagraph);
```

When you add a node to your web page by appending it as a child to a parent, as I did in the example above, the limitation is that you have no control over where the new element lands among the parent's children. JavaScript always places it at the end. So for example, if the div in the example above already has three paragraphs, the new paragraph will become the fourth one, even if you'd like to place it in a higher position.

The solution is **insertBefore**.

For example, suppose you want the paragraph to be the first one in the div, rather than the last.

```
1 var parentDiv = document.getElementById("div1");
2 var newParagraph = document.createElement("p");
3 var t = document.createTextNode("Hello world!");
4 newParagraph.appendChild(t);
5 paragraph1 = parentDiv.firstChild;
6 parentDiv.insertBefore(newParagraph, paragraph1);
```

The example above selects one of the children of the parent element as the target (line 5), and tells JavaScript to insert the new element and its text content before that element (line 6).

There is no **insertAfter** method as such. But you can still do it. Simply **insertBefore** the target node's next sibling.

```
1 var target = parentDiv.childNodes[1];
2 parentDiv.insertBefore(newE, target.nextSibling);
```

By inserting the new node before the next sibling of the second child, you insert the new node after the second child.

To remove a node, use **removeChild**.

```
1 var parentDiv = document.getElementById("div1");
2 var nodeToRemove = parentDiv.childNodes[2];
3 parentDiv.removeChild(nodeToRemove);
```

Find the interactive coding exercises for this chapter at http://www.ASmarterWayToLearn.com/js/68.html

69
Objects

I'm sure you've seen tables like this, comparing different packages offered by a webhost.

Hosting Plans			
	Basic	Professional	Ultimate
Monthly	$3.99	$5.99	$9.99
Disk Space	100 GB	500 GB	2000 GB
Data Transfer	1000 GB/Mo	5000 GB/Mo	20000 GB/Mo
Site Pages	10	50	500

If you wanted to use this data in JavaScript, you could assign each value to a different variable, like this.

```
1 var plan1Name = "Basic";
2 var plan1Price = 3.99;
3 var plan1Space = 100;
4 var plan1Data = 1000;
5 var plan1Pages = 10;
6 var plan2Name = "Professional";
7 var plan2Price = 5.99;
8 var plan2Space = 500;
9 var plan2Data = 5000;
10 var plan2Pages = 50;
11 var plan3Name = "Ultimate";
12 var plan3Price = 9.99;
13 var plan3Space = 2000;
14 var plan3Data = 20000;
15 var plan3Pages = 500;
```

Having made all these variable assignments, you could then, for example, write this JavaScript statement...

```
alert("The cost of the " + plan2Name + "package is $" +
plan2Price + " per month.");
```

...and an alert would display saying, "The cost of the Professional package is $5.99 per month."

But assigning all these values to variables is unwieldy, and can lead to problems if things get complicated. A better way to handle the situation is to create *objects* with *properties*. This is a handier scheme that more accurately reflects the 2-dimensional, grid-like nature of the host company's table that we started with. This table shows all the options expressed as objects and properties.

Object	plan1	plan2	plan3
name (a property)	"Basic"	"Professional"	"Ultimate"
price (a property)	3.99	5.99	9.99
space (a property)	100	500	2000
transfer (a property)	1000	5000	20000
pages (a property)	10	50	500

In this example, each hosting plan is an object—plan1, plan2, plan3. And each object has 5 properties—name, cost, space, transfer, and pages. Properties are just variables that are attached to an object. In this case, there's a string property (name) and four number properties (price, space, transfer, and pages) for each object.

In code we refer to objects and their properties using dot notation. Here's the statement that creates the alert shown above, with object-property pairs replacing the simple variables.

```
alert("The cost of the " + plan2.name + " package is $" +
plan2.price + " per month.");
```

plan2.name represents "Professional". **plan2.price** represents 5.99.

The most straightforward way to define an object and its properties is this.

```
1 var plan1 = {
2    name: "Basic",
3    price: 3.99,
4    space: 100,
5    transfer: 1000,
6    pages: 10
7 };
```

Things to notice:

- The code begins like any variable definition, with the keyword **var**, followed by the object name, and then an equal sign.

- But then, instead of a value, there's a curly bracket, whose twin comes at the end of the block.

- Each property begins with a name, followed by a colon, and then a value.

- Each property definition except the last ends with a comma.

- The closing curly bracket is followed by a semicolon, because of the equal sign in the first line.

Now let's add one more property, **discountMonths**. If the current month is July, August, or December, the customer gets a 20 percent discount on the hosting plan. To keep track of those special months, we'll assign them to a new property. This new property is an array, not a simple variable.

```
plan1.discountMonths = [6, 7, 11];
```

The statement above creates a new property of the object **plan1**, **discountMonths**, and assigns an array to it representing the three months when the customer gets a discount.

You refer to the individual elements of this array property the same way you'd refer to the elements of any array, with a number inside brackets, but using the dot notation of the object-property pair, **plan1.discountMonths**.

```
var mo = plan1.discountMonths[2];
```

The statement above assigns the third element of the array, the number representing December, to the variable mo.

So far, we've defined only one object, **plan1**, and its properties. To complete the set of objects that includes **plan2** and **plan3**, you'd have to do the same thing again, and then again. You may be thinking that this all takes more work than just defining 15 simple variables as I did early in the chapter, but defining objects and their properties is actually a better way to go, for reasons that I'll discuss in later chapters. Plus, there's a less labor-intensive way to go about it, which you'll also learn.

Find the interactive coding exercises for this chapter at http://www.ASmarterWayToLearn.com/js/69.html

70
Objects: Properties

To change the value of an object's property, use a simple assignment statement, the same way you'd assign a value to a plain variable.

```
deal3.cost = 79.95;
```

Whatever the value of **deal3.cost** was, now it's 79.95.
Of course, you can assign a string instead of a number.

```
deal3.name = "Super-saver";
```

Whatever the value of **deal3.name** was, now it's "Super-saver".
You can also assign an array list to a property.

```
deal3.features = ["Guarantee", "Free Ship"];
```

Whatever the value of **deal3.features** was, now it's an array with the elements "Guarantee" and "Free Ship."
You can also assign a Boolean value.

```
deal3.membersOnly = false;
```

Whatever the value of **deal3.membersOnly** was, now it's **false**.
You can also use an assignment statement to define a new property for an object. Suppose the object **deal3** has some properties, but none of them are **deal3.market**. Now you want to add it, while assigning it a value.

```
deal3.market = "regional";
```

Just as you can create an undefined variable by not assigning it a value, you can create an object without any properties.

```
var deal4 = {};
```

If you want to create a property now and assign it a value later, you can create it with a value of undefined.

```
deal3.market = undefined;
```

Note that the keyword **undefined** isn't in quotation marks. It isn't a string.

You can delete a property of an object.

```
delete deal3.market;
```

You can check to see if a property of an object exists. The following statement tests whether there is such a thing as **deal3.market** and assigns the result (**true** or **false**) to the variable **propertyExists**.

```
propertyExists = "market" in deal3;
```

Things to notice:

- You could use any legal variable name instead of **propertyExists**.

- The keyword **in** asks, "The property market is in the object **deal3**—true or false?"

- The property **market** is in quotes.

- The object **deal3** is not in quotes.

Find the interactive coding exercises for this chapter at http://www.ASmarterWayToLearn.com/js/70.html

71
Objects: Methods

Let's return to the chart showing different hosting plans.

Hosting Plans			
	Basic	**Professional**	**Ultimate**
Monthly	$3.99	$5.99	$9.99
Disk Space	100 GB	500 GB	2000 GB
Data Transfer	1000 GB/Mo	5000 GB/Mo	20000 GB/Mo
Site Pages	10	50	500
Discount mo	Jul, Aug	Jul, Aug, Dec	Jul, Aug

Note that I've added a new row at the bottom, for discount months offered for each plan. We're going to write a function that calculates the annual charge based on this chart. If the user signs up in certain months, he gets a discount for the entire year. If he signs up for the Basic plan in July or August, he gets 20 per cent off. If he signs up for the Professional plan in July, August, or December, he gets 20 per cent off. If he signs up for the Ultimate plan in July or August, he gets 20 per cent off.

We begin by creating three objects with properties. This is the object and its properties that represent the Basic plan.

```
1 var plan1 = {
2   name: "Basic",
3   price: 3.99,
4   space: 100,
5   transfer: 1000,
6   pages: 10,
7   discountMonths: [6, 7]
8 };
```

The function below cycles through all the discount months (line 5) checking to see if any of them happen to be the current month (line 6). If so, it calculates a 20 percent discount by multiplying the regular price by .8. Then it multiplies the monthly price, discounted or not, by 12, to get the annual price, and returns the number to the calling code (line 11).

```
1 function calcAnnual() {

2   var bestPrice = plan1.price;
3   var currDate = new Date();
4   var theMo = currDate.getMonth();
5   for (var i = 0; i < plan1.discountMonths.length; i++) {
6     if (plan1.discountMonths[i] === theMo) {
7       bestPrice = plan1.price * .8;
8       break;
9     }
10  }
11  return bestPrice * 12;
12 }
```

This is the calling statement that executes the function.

```
var annualPrice = calcAnnual();
```

But now let's make the function more flexible so the discount rate can vary, depending on the value that the calling statement passes to it. Here's the revision, with the percentage to be charged, passed to the parameter **percentIfDisc**, if the user qualifies for a discount.

```
1 function calcAnnual(percentIfDisc) {
2   var bestPrice = plan1.price;
3   var currDate = new Date();
4   var theMo = currDate.getMonth();
5   for (var i = 0; i < plan1.discountMonths.length; i++) {
6     if (plan1.discountMonths[i] === theMo) {
7       bestPrice = plan1.price * percentIfDisc;
8       break;
9     }
10  }
11  return bestPrice * 12;
12 }
```

This is the calling statement that passes the value to the function and executes it. In this example, it passes the value .85, representing a discount of 15 percent.

```
var annualPrice = calcAnnual(.85);
```

You've learned that you can attach a variable to an object, and the variable becomes the object's property. Here's more news. You can attach a function to an object, and the function becomes that object's *method*. It does the same task the regular function does, but now it's attached to an object. The reasons why you would want to use a method rather than an ordinary function will become clear in subsequent chapters. For now, let me show you how it's done.

This code inserts the function that I coded above into the object definition, so now it's a method. Operationally, it's the same as the plain-vanilla function, but now it's attached to the object.

```
1   var plan1 = {
2     name: "Basic",
3     price: 3.99,
4     space: 100,
5     transfer: 1000,
6     pages: 10,
7     discountMonths: [6, 7],
8     calcAnnual: function(percentIfDisc) {
9       var bestPrice = plan1.price;
10      var currDate = new Date();
11      var theMo = currDate.getMonth();
12      for (var i = 0; i < plan1.discountMonths.length;
i++) {
13        if (plan1.discountMonths[i] === theMo) {
14          bestPrice = plan1.price * percentIfDisc;
15          break;
16        }
17      }
18      return bestPrice * 12;
19    }
20 };
```

Things to notice:

- Except for the first line, every line of the method is identical to the code I used to create the plain-vanilla function that we started with.

- The method definition begins the same way a property definition begins, with the name followed by a colon.

- A comma ends every property definition and method definition except for the last property or method. If you were to add a property or method below the **calcAnnual** method definition, you'd need to insert a comma after the closing curly bracket of the **calcAnnual** definition.

- The parentheses that indicate that a variable name is the name of a function come immediately after the keyword **function**. Parameters, if there are any, go inside the parentheses, as in any function definition.

This is how you'd call the method.

```
var annualPrice = plan1.calcAnnual(.85);
```

I'm going to add a refinement to the method definition. In the definition I coded above, the properties are referred to using the name of the object—for example, **plan1.price**. This works, but a better approach, for reasons that will become clear in subsequent chapters, is to replace the name of the object with the keyword **this**. When JavaScript sees this keyword, it knows you're referring to the object that's being defined.

```
1   var plan1 = {
2     name: "Basic",
3     price: 3.99,
4     space: 100,
5     transfer: 1000,
6     pages: 10,
7     discountMonths: [6, 7],
8     calcAnnual: function(percentIfDisc) {
9       var bestPrice = this.price;
10      var currDate = new Date();
11      var theMo = currDate.getMonth();
12      for (var i = 0; i < this.discountMonths.length; i++)
{
13        if (this.discountMonths[i] === theMo) {
14          bestPrice = this.price * percentIfDisc;
15          break;
16        }
17      }
18      return bestPrice * 12;
19    }
20  };
```

When you write **this.whatever**, JavaScript is smart enough to understand that you're referring to a property of the object that's being defined—in this case, **plan1**.

Find the interactive coding exercises for this chapter at http://www.ASmarterWayToLearn.com/js/71.html

72
Objects: Constructors

Again, here's a version of the chart showing different hosting plans.

Hosting Plans			
	Basic	**Professional**	**Ultimate**
Monthly	$3.99	$5.99	$9.99
Disk Space	100 GB	500 GB	2000 GB
Data Transfer	1000 GB/Mo	5000 GB/Mo	20000 GB/Mo
Site Pages	10	50	500

This is how I encapsulated the information for the Basic plan in an object and five properties.

```
1 var plan1 = {
2   name: "Basic",
3   price: 3.99,
4   space: 100,
5   transfer: 1000,
6   pages: 10
7 };
```

But that only gets us an object that represents the first plan. I'd have to do the same thing again for the Professional and Ultimate plans. This is too much hand craftsmanship. We need a factory to crank out these things by the dozen. JavaScript lets you build such a factory. It's called a *constructor function*.

```
1 function Plan(name, price, space, transfer, pages) {
2   this.name = name;
3   this.price = price;
4   this.space = space;
5   this.transfer = transfer;
6   this.pages = pages;
7 }
```

This would be a plain-vanilla function definition but for two differences:

- The function name is capitalized. JavaScript doesn't care whether you do this or not, but it's conventional to do it to distinguish constructor functions from regular functions.

- Each of the parameter values is assigned to a variable. But the variable is a property attached to some object whose name hasn't been specified yet. But don't worry. Just as the parameter values will be filled in by the calling code, so will the name of the object.

This is the calling code that creates the object for the Basic plan.

```
var plan1 = new Plan("Basic", 3.99, 100, 1000, 10);
```

This would be just a regular function call if it weren't for that **new**. It's the keyword that tells JavaScript to create a new object. The name of the new object is **plan1**. Its properties are enumerated inside the parentheses.

Now it's easy to mass-produce as many objects as you want, using the same pattern.

```
1 var plan1 = new Plan("Basic", 3.99, 100, 1000, 10);
2 var plan2 = new Plan("Premium", 5.99, 500, 5000, 50);
3 var plan3 = new Plan("Ultimate", 9.99, 2000, 20000, 500);
```

It's common to use the same names for parameters and properties, but you don't have to. You could write:

```
1 function Plan(name, price, space, transfer, pages) {
2    this.doc = name;
3    this.grumpy = price;
4    this.sleepy = space;
5    this.bashful = transfer;
6    this.sneezy = pages;
7 }
```

Find the interactive coding exercises for this chapter at http://www.ASmarterWayToLearn.com/js/72.html

73
Objects: Constructors for methods

Here's the version of the hosting chart that includes discount months.

Hosting Plans			
	Basic	**Professional**	**Ultimate**
Monthly	$3.99	$5.99	$9.99
Disk Space	100 GB	500 GB	2000 GB
Data Transfer	1000 GB/Mo	5000 GB/Mo	20000 GB/Mo
Site Pages	10	50	500
Discount mo	Jul, Aug	Jul, Aug, Dec	Jul, Aug

In Chapter 71 I showed you how to attach a function to an object, using the same approach you use when you attach a variable to an object. When you attach a variable to an object, it's called a property of the object. When you attach a function to an object, it's called a method of the object. In the example below, the method checks to see if the current date is in a discount month and, if so, applies the discount. Then the method calculates the annual charge.

If you're creating more than one object with the same pattern of properties and methods, it's a convenience to build the method as well as the properties into the constructor function.

In the following code, the constructor creates the same method for every object that is created, as it creates all the properties for each object.

```
1 function Plan(name, price, space, transfer, pages,
discountMonths) {
2     this.name = name;
3     this.price = price;
4     this.space = space;
5     this.transfer = transfer;
6     this.pages = pages;
7     this.discountMonths = discountMonths;
8     this.calcAnnual = function(percentIfDisc) {
9       var bestPrice = this.price;
10      var currDate = new Date();
11      var theMo = currDate.getMonth();
12      for (var i = 0; i < this.discountMonths.length; i++)
{
13        if (this.discountMonths[i] === theMo) {
14          bestPrice = this.price * percentIfDisc;"
15          break;"
16        }
17      }
18      return bestPrice * 12;
19    };
20 }
```

Things to notice about line 8, the beginning of the method definition:

- Like the property definitions above it, the line begins with the keyword **this**, referring to the name of whatever object is being constructed at any given time.
- The next three pieces are the same: a dot, the name of the method, and an equal sign.
- The next piece is different: the keyword **function**.
- In this case, a single parameter is inside the parentheses, **percentIfDisc**. This is not a parameter that's part of the constructor. It's a parameter of the method that the constructor will create for each object. A value is passed to it not when a new object is created using the constructor, but when the method, having already been created along with its object via the constructor, is called.

This is the code that calls the constructor function to create three new objects that correspond to the three hosting plans.

```
1 var p1 = new Plan("Basic", 3.99, 100, 1000, 10, [6, 7]);
2 var p2 = new Plan("Premium", 5.99, 500, 5000, 50, [6, 7, 11]);
3 var p3 = new Plan("Ultimate", 9.99, 2000, 20000, 500, [6, 7]);
```

Once the objects and their properties and method are created by the code above, this is the code that calls, for example, the method for the Premium plan.

```
var annualPrice = p2.calcAnnual(.85);
```

The main difference between the method definition in the one-off literal object definition (no constructor) and the method definition in the constructor function is the first line. In other respects, the two definitions are identical.

This is the first line of a method definition when an object is created on a one-off basis without a constructor:

```
calcAnnual: function(percentIfDisc) {
```

This is the first line of a method definition within a constructor:

```
this.calcAnnual = function(percentIfDisc) {
```

There are two other differences. Because in the constructor function the method definition begins with an assignment (something = something else), you need a semicolon after the closing curly bracket. And no comma is necessary if another property or method definition follows.

Find the interactive coding exercises for this chapter at http://www.ASmarterWayToLearn.com/js/73.html

74
Objects: Prototypes

In the last chapter you created three objects using a constructor. Each object corresponded to a hosting plan. Each object had six properties and one method. Here's a chart showing the three objects and their properties and method. Check out the last row, shaded in the table, the one representing the methods for the three objects...

Object	plan1	plan2	plan3
name (a property)	"Basic"	"Professional"	"Ultimate"
price (a property)	3.99	5.99	9.99
space (a property)	100	500	2000
transfer (a property)	1000	5000	20000
pages (a property)	10	50	500
discountMonths (a property)	Jul, Aug	Jul, Aug, Dec	Jul, Aug
calcAnnual (a method)	Calculates annual charge	Calculates annual charge	Calculates annual charge

There's something inelegant about the shaded last row. The properties shown in the rows above it are customized for each object, but the method is always the same from object to object. The constructor function keeps duplicating the same method for each object, object after object. If we were to create 100 objects using the constructor, JavaScript would duplicate the same method 100 times, once for each object. It would work, but it ain't pretty. This table, which shows all of the objects sharing a single method, makes more sense.

Object	plan1	plan2	plan3
name (a property)	"Basic"	"Professional"	"Ultimate"
price (a property)	3.99	5.99	9.99
space (a property)	100	500	2000
transfer (a property)	1000	5000	20000
pages (a property)	10	50	500
discountMonths (a property)	Jul, Aug	Jul, Aug, Dec	Jul, Aug
calcAnnual (a method)	Calculates annual charge (shared by all objects)		

We want only one copy of the method, shared by all objects created with the constructor, no matter how many objects are created. How do we do it? With a *prototype* statement.

First, we don't include the method in the constructor function, because that creates a copy of the method for every single object that's created with the constructor. Instead, we define the method as a prototype of the constructor, this way.

```
1  Plan.prototype.calcAnnual = function(percentIfDisc) {
2    var bestPrice = this.price;
3    var currDate = new Date();
4    var theMo = currDate.getMonth();
5    for (var i = 0; i < this.discountMonths.length; i++) {
6      if (this.discountMonths[i] === theMo) {
7        bestPrice = this.price * percentIfDisc;
8        break;
9      }
10   }
11   return bestPrice * 12;
12 };
```

Now, all objects created with the constructor **Plan** will share the same copy of the method **calcAnnual**. There's no unnecessary duplication.

Note that except for the first line, the method is coded exactly as I coded it when it was part of the constructor definition. Even the first line is the same, if you consider only the parts on the right side of the equal sign. The parts on the left side, connected by dots, are:

- the name of the constructor function, in this case **Plan**

- the keyword **prototype**

- the name of the method that all objects created with **Plan** will share, in this case **calcAnnual**

Objects can have prototype properties as well as prototype methods. Suppose you wanted all objects created with **Plan** to share the same property, **cancellable**, with a value of **true**. The code:

```
Plan.prototype.cancellable = true;
```

Now all objects created with the constructor function **Plan** share a property, **cancellable**, whose value is **true**. This is how the object table looks with the prototype method and the prototype property.

Object	plan1	plan2	plan3
name (a property)	"Basic"	"Professional"	"Ultimate"
price (a property)	3.99	5.99	9.99
space (a property)	100	500	2000
transfer (a property)	1000	5000	20000
pages (a property)	10	50	500
discountMonths (a property)	Jul, Aug	Jul, Aug, Dec	Jul, Aug
calcAnnual (a method)	Calculates annual charge (shared by all objects)		
cancellable (a property)	true (shared by all objects)		

It's possible to override a prototype for any individual object. For example, suppose you want all objects created with the constructor to share the same cancellable property, except for the least expensive plan, plan1, with the name "Basic." This is the statement that does it.

```
plan1.cancellable = false;
```

All objects created with the constructor still share the property **cancellable**, but now the value of that property for one object is different from all the others. Here's the chart.

Object	plan1	plan2	plan3
name (a property)	"Basic"	"Professional"	"Ultimate"
price (a property)	3.99	5.99	9.99
space (a property)	100	500	2000
transfer (a property)	1000	5000	20000
pages (a property)	10	50	500
discountMonths (a property)	Jul, Aug	Jul, Aug, Dec	Jul, Aug
calcAnnual (a method)	Calculates annual charge (shared by all objects)		
cancellable (a property)	Exception: this one's false	true (shared by all objects with 1 exception)	

In the same way, you could override a shared prototype method for any individual objects as well.

Find the interactive coding exercises for this chapter at http://www.ASmarterWayToLearn.com/js/74.html

75
Objects:
Checking for properties and methods

You can check to see if an object has a particular property by writing a simple statement like this.

```
var gotTheProperty = "price" in plan1;
```

Here are the parts:

- the property in question, enclosed in quotes—in this case, **price**

- the keyword **in**

- the object, in this case, **plan1**

Again, the question is, does the object named **plan1** have a property called **price**? In other words, is there such a thing as **plan1.price**? In the example of three hosting plans that we've been using, **plan1** does have a price, 3.99. So **gotTheProperty** is assigned **true**. But **plan1** doesn't have a property named **location**. So if we write...

```
var gotTheProperty = "location" in plan1;
```

...the variable **gotTheProperty** is **false**.

plan1 in the example also has a method named **calcAnnual**. A method is a type of property of an object, so if you write...

```
var gotTheProperty = "calcAnnual" in plan1;
```

...the variable **gotTheProperty** is **true**.

Things to notice:

- The property, a variable, is enclosed in quotation marks. We're not used to putting JavaScript variables inside quotation marks, so this is something to make a note of.

- The keyword is **in**—pretty intuitive. The code asks, "Is there a property called 'price' in **plan1**?"

Here's how to get a list of the object's properties:

```
1 var listOfProperties = [];
2 for (var prop in plan1) {
3   listOfProperties.push(prop);
4 }
```

Line 1 declares an empty array, **listOfProperties**. Lines 2-4 cycle through all the properties of **plan1**, adding each property (**push**), including any methods, to the array **listOfProperties**. The array **listOfProperties** winds up with a value of "name,price,space,transfer,pages,discountMonths,calcAnnual".

Note that, unlike a regular *for* loop, this one doesn't establish a limit on the number of loops or increment a counter. After each iteration, JavaScript automatically moves to the next property of the object and stops iterating when there are no more properties to enumerate.

Instead of **prop**, you could use any other legal variable name.

The method, **calcAnnual**, wasn't included in the original definition of the object **plan1**. It was later added to the prototype of the constructor function that I used to create the object, so became a property of the object *by inheritance*. The code above includes inherited properties (including methods) in the collection. To limit the list of properties to those explicitly declared for the object, omitting those that are inherited from a prototype, use **hasOwnProperty**.

```
1 var listOfProperties = [];
2 for (var prop in plan1) {
3   if (plan1.hasOwnProperty(prop)) {
4     listOfProperties.push(prop);
5   }
6 }
```

In the example above, each property in turn is assigned to the variable **prop**. Then the *if* statement tests to see if it's a property owned by the object as opposed to being inherited through a prototype.

You can test a literal property name instead of using a variable.

```
var isOwnedProperty = plan1.hasOwnProperty("price");
```

Find the interactive coding exercises for this chapter at http://www.ASmarterWayToLearn.com/js/75.html

76
Browser control: Getting and setting the URL

In addition to making things happen on the webpage, you can use JavaScript to control the browser. To begin with, you can get the browser to tell you its current location.

```
var whereWeAt = window.location.href;
```

For example, if the browser is currently at *http://www.mybeautifulsite.com/products/page33.html#humidifier*, the statement above will assign the string "http://www.mybeautifulsite.com/products/page33.html#humidifier" to the variable **whereWeAt**.

You can also get pieces of this. This statement gets just the domain name.

```
var theDomain = window.location.hostname;
```

In the example, the string "www.mybeautifulwebsite.com" is assigned to the variable **theDomain**. "http://", the path, and the anchor are omitted.

Here's how you get the path.

```
var thePath = window.location.pathname;
```

In the example, the string "/products/page33.html" is assigned to the variable **thePath**. If the browser were on the home page and the URL were simply http://www.mybeautifulsite.com, the string "/" would be assigned to the variable.

In the example, the browser has been pointed to a section of the page marked by the anchor #*humidifier*. This statement identifies the anchor.

```
var theAnchor = window.location.hash;
```

The string "#humidifier" is assigned to the variable **theAnchor**. If there is no anchor in the URL, the variable is assigned an empty string, "".

As usual, you can reverse the order of things, telling the browser where to go instead of asking where it is.

```
window.location.href = "http://www.me.com/1.html";
```

The statement above tells the browser to navigate to the page named *1.html* at the site *me.com*.

If you wanted the browser to navigate to the site's home page, you'd write...

```
window.location.href = "http://www.me.com";
```

And if you wanted it to land on an anchor...

```
window.location.href = "http://www.me.com/1.html#section9";
```

It would be nice if you could use **window.pathname** = ... to move to a different page on the current site or **window.hash** = ... to move to an anchor on the current page, but you can't. What you can do, though, is query the browser for the domain name and combine that with the page where you want to go.

```
1 var currentSite = window.location.hostname;
2 var destination = "http://" + currentSite + "/wow.html";
3 window.location.href = destination;
```

Here's the line-by-line breakdown:

1. Gets the domain name and assigns it to the variable **currentSite**. Example: www.me.com

2. Concatenates the string "http://" with the domain name plus the destination page and assigns the combo to the variable **destination**

3. Directs the browser to the destination

This is how to direct the browser to an anchor on the current page.

```
1 var currentSite = window.location.hostname;
2 var currentPath = window.location.pathname;
3 var destination = "http://" + currentSite + currentPath +
"#humidifier";
4 window.location.href = destination;
```

Here's the breakdown:

1. Gets the domain name and assigns it to the variable currentSite. Example: www.me.com

2. Gets the pathname and assigns it to the variable currentPath. Example: /1.html

3. Concatenates the string "http://" with the domain name, the destination page, and the desired anchor and assigns the combo to the variable **destination**

4. Directs the browser to the destination

Coding Alternatives to Be Aware Of

- You can omit **window**. It's legal to use **location.href**, **location.hostname**, **location.pathname**, and **location.hash**. It's more common to include **window**.

- You can omit **href** when you're detecting the URL. It's legal to use **window.location**, or simply **location**. (See above.) Including **href** is preferred for esoteric reasons.

- You can use **document.URL** as an alternative to **window.location.href**

- There are two more ways to direct the browser to a url, alternatives to **window.location.href**. You'll learn how to use these in the next chapter.

Find the interactive coding exercises for this chapter at http://www.ASmarterWayToLearn.com/js/76.html

77
Browser control:
Getting and setting the URL another way

In the last chapter you learned to direct the browser to a new URL by assigning a string to **window.location.href**. Here's another way to do the same thing.

```
window.location.assign("http://www.me.com");
```

The statement directs the browser to the home page of *me.com*.

As with the **window.location.href** statement, you can make the URL as detailed as you like.

```
window.location.assign("http://www.me.com/lojack.html#guara
ntee");
```

The statement directs the browser to the anchor *#guarantee* on the *lojack.html* page of the site *me.com*.

Here's another alternative that has a slightly different effect.

```
window.location.replace("http://www.me.com/lojack.html#guar
antee");
```

Once again, the statement directs the browser to a new URL. But by using **replace** instead of **assign**, you interfere with the browser history. When you use **assign**, the history is intact. The statement takes the user away from the original page, to the new page. If, after arriving at the new page, she presses the **Backspace** key or clicks the browser's **back** button, she goes back to the original page that she just came from. But when you use **replace**, the original page doesn't make it into the history. If the user presses **Backspace** after being taken to the new page, she's taken to the page that displayed before the original page since the original page is no longer in the history. If there is no page before the original page, nothing happens when she presses **Backspace**.

To reload the current page code one of these statements:

```
window.location.reload(true);
window.location.reload(false);
window.location.reload();
```

All three statements reload the current page. If the argument is **true** (example 1 above), the statement forces the browser to load the page from the server. If the argument is **false** (example 2) or if there is no argument (example 3), the browser will load the page from the cache if the page has been cached.

Coding Alternatives to Be Aware Of

You can use **window.location.href = window.location.href** or any of the abbreviated alternatives to reload the current page. The reload is faster, but it doesn't allow you to specify whether the browser reloads from the server or the cache. **document.URL = document.URL** doesn't work.

Find the interactive coding exercises for this chapter at http://www.ASmarterWayToLearn.com/js/77.html

78
Browser control: Forward and reverse

You can make the browser go back one URL in the browser history, as if the user has pressed the **Backspace** key or clicked the browser's **back** button.

```
history.back();
```

To make the browser go forward in the history, as if the user has pressed **alt-right-arrow** or clicked the browser's **forward** button...

```
history.forward();
```

In both cases, if there is no URL in the history that would make the move possible, the browser does nothing.

You can tell the browser how many steps in the history you want to take, using negative numbers to go back and positive numbers to go forward. The following statement is the equivalent of pressing the **Backspace** key three times.

```
history.go(-3);
```

The following statement sends the browser forward two URLs.

```
history.go(2);
```

If a negative number inside the parentheses is greater than the number of previous URLs in the history, the browser will do nothing. If a positive number inside the parentheses is greater than the number of forward URLs in the history, the browser will do nothing.

When you want to go forward or backward just one step, you can choose either method..

```
history.back();
```

...is the same as...

```
history.go(-1);
```

And...

```
history.forward();
```

...is the same as...

```
history.go(1);
```

There is no reliable way to find out how many items, backward and forward, there are in the history.

If the user clicked a link to get to the current page, you can get the URL of the page where the link was clicked.

```
var whereUserCameFrom = document.referrer;
```

The statement above assigns the URL where the link was clicked to the variable **whereUserCameFrom**.

However, this works only if a link was clicked, including a link in a search result. If the user got to your page through a bookmark or by entering your URL in the address bar, the result of **document.referrer** will be an empty string, "".

Find the interactive coding exercises for this chapter at http://www.ASmarterWayToLearn.com/js/78.html

79
Browser control: Filling the window with content

Popup windows aren't popular, but have their legitimate uses. To use them, you'll have to deal with popup blockers, which you'll learn to do shortly. First let me teach you the code that creates the window.

This is the basic, barebones statement.

```
var monkeyWindow = window.open();
```

The code above opens a blank window of maximum size and gives it a *handle*, a variable that refers to this particular window—in this case, **monkeyWindow**. Depending on the browser, the window may open on top of the previous window, in a new tab, or even in a new copy of the browser. You can't control this.

You can use the **write** method to fill a window with content.

```
1 var monkeyWindow = window.open();
2 var windowContent = "<h1>Capuchin monkey</h1><img src=
'monkey.jpg'><p>The word capuchin derives from a group of
friars<br>named the Order of Friars Minor Capuchin who
wear<br>brown robes with large hoods covering their
heads.</p>";
3 monkeyWindow.document.write(windowContent);
```

Here's the line-by-line breakdown:

1. Opens a new window and assigns it the handle **monkeyWindow**

2. Assigns text to the variable **windowContent**

3. Fills the window with the text

Things to notice:

- Inside the main quotes that enclose the whole string, any quoted text must be in single quotes, as in **<img src='monkey.jpg'>**.

- Using the **document.write** method, you place the HTML string on the page. You specify the window's handle, the variable that you declared when you opened the window.

- The **document.write** method in this example is used to fill an empty window with content. You could also use it to write to a window that already has content, overwriting all the HTML of the original document, replacing its content.

- Instead of assigning the HTML string to a variable and specifying the variable inside the parentheses, you could just put the HTML string inside the parentheses, enclosed in quotes of course. But this would be even more unwieldy than the example code.

The second way to fill the window with content is to assign a document to it, as you learned to do in previous chapters.

```
monkeyWindow.location.assign("http://www.animals.com/capuch
in.html");
```

...or...

```
monkeyWindow.location.href =
"http://www.animals.com/capuchin.html";
```

The third and most common way to fill the window with content is to include the document assignment in the statement that opens the window.

```
var monkeyWindow =
window.open("http://www.animals.com/capuchin.html");
```

If the document you're opening in the popup shares the same host and directory as the original document, you can just write...

```
var monkeyWindow = window.open("capuchin.html");
```

This is how you close a window.

```
monkeyWindow.close();
```

Find the interactive coding exercises for this chapter at http://www.ASmarterWayToLearn.com/js/79.html

80
Browser control: The window's size and location

In the last chapter you learned to open a new window without parameters—a full-size window—and how to open a window with a single parameter—a URL.

A second parameter that you can include is a window name.

```
var monkeyWindow = window.open("monk.html", "win1");
```

The second item in the parentheses, "win1", is the name— useful for specifying the target attribute of an **<a>** or **<form>** element in HTML.

Things to know:

- The name, used in HTML, is not the handle. The handle is used in JavaScript statements that write to the window, assign a URL to it, or close it. The handle is the variable that precedes the equal sign.

- The name is in quotes.

- The name is separated from the URL by a comma followed by a space.

- The name itself can't have spaces in it.

You can specify a URL parameter without a name parameter, but you can't specify a name parameter without a URL parameter. But it is okay to specify an empty URL parameter, like this.

```
var monkeyWindow = window.open("", "win1");
```

Often, you'll want to specify a window size.

```
var monkeyWindow = window.open("monk.html", "win1",
"width=420,height=380");
```

Things to know:

- Both parameters, width and height, are enclosed by a single set of quotation marks.

- The absence of spaces within the quotation marks isn't a mere style preference but a requirement. Any spaces here will break JavaScript.

- The numbers refer to pixels. In the example above, the window will be 420 pixels wide and 380 pixels high.

- Width and height must be a minimum of 100.

- Unlike the URL and name parameters, the order doesn't matter. Width can come before height, height can come before width. But the width-and-height set must come third, after URL and name.

- In order to specify these parameters, you must specify a URL and name, even if you specify empty strings.

A window that's smaller than the screen will display in the upper-left corner of the screen. But you can optionally tell the browser where to place the window.

```
var w = window.open("", "",
"width=420,height=380,left=200,top=100");
```

Things to know:

- Again, the numbers are pixels—number of pixels from the left edge of the screen and number of pixels from the top of the screen.

- The positioning parameters are included within the same set of quotation marks as the size parameters, and, like the size parameters, are separated by a comma and no space.

- The parameter order within the quotation marks doesn't matter.

- You can specify window size without specifying window position, but if you specify window position without size, it will be ignored since it will be a full-size window that fills the whole screen.

As usual, some or all of the parameters can be assigned to a variable, and the variable can be used in the statement that opens the window. Since the whole thing has to be a quoted string, the quotes within the string have to be changed to single quotes.

```
1 var windowSpecs = "'faq.html', 'faq',
'width=420,height=380,left=200,top=100'";
2 var faqPage = window.open(windowSpecs);
```

Find the interactive coding exercises for this chapter at http://www.ASmarterWayToLearn.com/js/80.html

81
Browser control: Testing for popup blockers

Popup blockers are now a standard feature of browsers, with some level of popup blocking usually built in as a default. JavaScript popups, and especially those that open a new page within the same website, are often tolerated by default, but you can never be sure. If popups are an essential feature of your site, you need to test whether your popups are going to be blocked. If they are, you can ask the user to disable the popup blocker for your site.

The test is pretty inelegant. You attempt to open a small test popup, then quickly close it—so fast that the user may not notice the little screen flash. If the attempt succeeds, the window's handle will have a value. If the popup is blocked, the handle will be **null**, and you can deliver your message to the user.

Here's the code.

```
1 function checkForPopBlocker() {
2    var testPop = window.open("",
"","width=100,height=100");
3    if (testPop === null) {
4      alert("Please disable your popup blocker.");
5    }
6    testPop.close();
7 }
```

Here's the line-by-line breakdown:

2 Attempts to open a tiny window

3-4 If the handle is assigned **null**, meaning the window couldn't open, an alert displays

6 Closes the window

The function shown above works with all browsers except Internet Explorer. In Internet Explorer, if the popup is blocked, the handle will be "undefined" instead of **null**. So to cover all bases, you need to code the function this way.

```
1 function checkForPopBlocker() {
2   var testPop = window.open("",
"","width=100,height=100");
3   if (testPop === null || typeof(testPop) ===
"undefined") {
4     alert("Please disable your popup blocker.");
5   }
6   testPop.close();
7 }
```

Normally, you'd run the test when the page loads.

```
<body onLoad="checkForPopBlocker();">
```

Find the interactive coding exercises for this chapter at http://www.ASmarterWayToLearn.com/js/81.html

82
Form validation: text fields

Is the user filling out your forms correctly? JavaScript helps you find out—that is, helps you *validate* your form. With form validation, if there's a problem, you can ask the user to try again. To begin with, if you have a required field, you can check to see if the user has entered something in it. Let's start with a simple form that asks the user to enter her last name.

Here's some markup for the form. I'm omitting lots of things, including styling stuff, to keep you focused on what's important to learn here.

```
<form onSubmit="return checkForLastName();">
  Please enter your last name.<br>
  <input type="text" id="lastNameField">
  <input type="submit" value="Submit Form">
</form>
```

When the user clicks the **Submit** button, the function **checkForLastName** is called.

Here's the function.

```
1 function checkForLastName() {
2    if
(document.getElementById("lastNameField").value.length ===
0) {
3       alert("Please enter your last name");
4       return false;
5    }
6 }
```

Line 2 asks whether the length of the value found in the field with the id "lastNameField" is 0. That is, is nothing entered there? If so, an alert displays asking the user to enter her name. And then in line 4 something else happens. The Boolean value **false** is returned to the calling code. This prevents the form from being submitted. In order for the submission to be called off, there has to be a matching keyword **return** in the markup that calls the function. Without this **return** in the calling code, the **return** in line 4 of the function won't stop the form from being submitted.

```
<form onSubmit="return checkForLastName();">
```

As a user-friendly touch, you can use the **focus** method to place the cursor in the field that needs to be completed.

```
1 function checkForLastName() {
2    if
(document.getElementById("lastNameField").value.length ===
0) {
3       alert("Please enter your last name");
4       document.getElementById("lastNameField").focus();
5       return false;
6    }
7 }
```

Repeating the **document.getElementById**... designation gets pretty unwieldy, so let's put it into a variable.

```
1 function checkForLastName() {
2    var targetField =
document.getElementById("lastNameField");
3    if (targetField.value.length === 0) {
4       alert("Please enter your last name");
5       targetField.focus();
6       return false;
7    }
8 }
```

Let's add one more feature. We'll direct the user's attention to the field that needs to be completed by giving it a yellow background color.

This requires two additional statements. If the user hasn't completed the field, line 6 changes its background color to yellow. After the user completes the field, line 9 restores the background color to white when the function runs again on the user's subsequent submission.

```
1   function checkForLastName() {2     var targetField =
document.getElementById("lastNameField");
3     if (targetField.value.length === 0) {
4       alert("Please enter your last name");
5       targetField.focus();
6       targetField.style.background = "yellow";
7       return false;
8     }
9     targetField.style.background = "white";10 }
```

Coding Alternatives to Be Aware Of

- The sample code in this chapter targets forms and fields by ID, which is the most straightforward approach. But you could target by name, by tag, or by position in the DOM hierarchy.

- Instead of hard-wiring the ID into the function, you could potentially make it multi-use by naming the field ID as a parameter, and passing the ID to it from the calling code.

Find the interactive coding exercises for this chapter at http://www.ASmarterWayToLearn.com/js/82.html

83
Form validation: drop-downs

Consider a form with a select-a-state field. I'm going to limit the list of states to just 4, for simplicity. When the user clicks the up or down arrow to the right of SELECT A STATE, a menu drops down. She selects a state from it.

But what happens if she forgets to select a state?

Here's the markup, simplified for teaching purposes.

```
<form onSubmit="return checkForSelection();">
  <select id="states">
    <option value="" selected="selected">
      SELECT A STATE</option>
        <option value="AL">Alabama</option>
        <option value="AK">Alaska</option>
        <option value="AZ">Arizona</option>
        <option value="AR">Arkansas</option>
      </select>  
  <input type="submit" value="Submit Form">
</form>
```

When the **Submit** button is clicked, the function **checkForSelection** is called. Note that once again, the keyword **return** precedes the function call.

Here's the function.

```
1 function checkForSelection() {
2   if (document.getElementById("states").selectedIndex ===
0) {
3     alert("Please select a state.");
4     return false;
5   }
6 }
```

In the function, if **selectedIndex** is 0 (line 2), it means the user hasn't made a selection. Line 3 displays an alert asking her to select. Line 4 returns **false**, cancelling the form submission.

Here's the function, revised two ways. First, it accepts the element ID as a parameter, allowing it to process more than one form. Second, the element is assigned to a variable.

```
1 function checkForSelection(selecID) {
2    var target = document.getElementById(selecID);
3    if (target.selectedIndex === 0) {
4       alert("Please select a state.");
5       return false;
6    }
7 }
```

The function coded above needs the event-handler to include the ID as an argument.

```
<form onSubmit="return checkForSelection('states');">
```

Find the interactive coding exercises for this chapter at http://www.ASmarterWayToLearn.com/js/83.html

84
Form validation: radio buttons

Let's code a form with a group of radio buttons. The buttons are Cat, Bat, and Hat.

This is the markup, simplified to keep your focus on what you're learning here.

```
<form onSubmit="return validateRadios();">
  <input type="radio" name="r1" value="cat"> Cat<br>
  <input type="radio" name="r1" value="bat"> Bat<br>
  <input type="radio" name="r1" value="hat"> Hat<br>
  <input type="submit" value="Submit Form"></form>
```

Note that the radio buttons all have the same name, "r1".

This is the validating function that checks to see if the user has clicked one of the buttons.

```
1   function validateRadios() {
2     var radios = document.getElementsByName("r1");
3     for (var i = 0; i < radios.length; i++)  {
4       if (radios[i].checked) {
5         return true;
6       }
7     }
8     alert("Please check one.");
9     return false;
10  }
```

Line 2 makes a collection of all the buttons with the name "r1" and assigns the collection to the variable **radios**. This is possible because, though an element can't share its id with any other elements, any number of elements can share the same name. Lines 3 and 7 loop through collection to see whether any of the buttons is checked. If so, the code breaks out of the function with the **return** keyword in line 5, passing back the Boolean **true** so the form can be submitted. If the loop runs its course without finding any buttons checked, line 8 displays an alert and line 9 returns **false**, cancelling the form submission.

The function can be used to validate button sections for any number of forms if we specify a parameter, allowing the event-handler to pass the button group name to the function.

```
1 function validateRadios(ename) {
2   var radios = document.getElementsByName(eName);
```

In order to use the function coded above, the event-handler would have to include the button group name as an argument.

```
<form onSubmit="return validateRadios('r1');">
```

Find the interactive coding exercises for this chapter at http://www.ASmarterWayToLearn.com/js/84.html

85
Form validation: ZIP codes

Now, a one-field form that asks the user to enter her ZIP code.

You've already learned how to make sure the user hasn't left the field blank. But how do you test whether she's entered the right number of digits for a ZIP—5 digits?

HTML gives you a way to keep her from entering too many digits: **maxlength=5**. But if you want to make sure she hasn't entered too few digits, you need to use JavaScript. Here's the function.

```
1 function validateZIP() {
2   var numChars =
document.getElementById("zip").value.length;
3   if (numChars < 5) {
4     alert("Please enter a 5-digit code.");
5     return false;
6   }
7 }
```

If the number of characters in the field is fewer than 5, an alert displays and **false** is returned to the calling code, cancelling the form submission.

Another question to ask about the ZIP field entry is whether the user has entered only numbers. Here's the additional code for that.

```
1  function validateZIP() {
2     var valueEntered =
document.getElementById("zip").value;
3     var numChars = valueEntered.length;
4     if (numChars < 5) {
5        alert("Please enter a 5-digit code.");
6        return false;
7     }
8     for (var i = 0; i <= 4; i++) {
9        var thisChar = parseInt(valueEntered[i]);
10       if (isNaN(thisChar)) {
11          alert("Please enter only numbers.");
12          return false;
13       }
14    }
15 }
```

The highlighted code loops through the five characters that have been entered, checking to make sure that all the characters are string characters representing numbers. Because the five characters in the field are string characters, each one has to be converted to a number if possible before being tested. Line 9 does this. Line 10 tests to see whether the attempted conversion worked. If a number resulted from **parseInt** in line 9, no problem. But if the character isn't a number after the conversion attempt—if it **isNaN** in line 10—an alert displays and **false** is returned, cancelling the form submission.

Coding Alternatives to Be Aware Of

A more elegant and more versatile way to validate forms is to use *regular expressions*. Regular expressions are outside the scope of this book, but I'll give you a small taste of them in the next chapter.

Find the interactive coding exercises for this chapter at http://www.ASmarterWayToLearn.com/js/85.html

86
Form validation: email

Validating an email field includes checking to make sure there are no illegal characters, like spaces, and that all the essentials of a legal email address are there: one or more characters, followed by @, followed by one or more characters, followed by a dot, followed by two to four characters. The standard way to test for all this is to match the user's entry with a regular expression. Regular expressions are beyond the scope of this book, but I'll give you a taste of them at the end of the chapter. Meanwhile, here's how to head off many user errors by using **indexOf**.

Let's start by checking for spaces, which are illegal in an email address.

```
1 function validateEmail() {
2    var eEntered = document.getElementById("email").value;
3    if (eEntered.indexOf(" ") !== -1) {4       alert("No
spaces allowed in address");
5       return false;
6    }
7 }
```

Line 3 is the key here. If the index of the illegal space character is anything other than -1, it means the character is in there somewhere, and an alert displays.

If you wanted to, you could test for the presence of all the other illegal characters the same way. But in that case, you'd be better off using a regular expression, as I show at the end of this chapter.

In an email address you want to see the @ sign at least one character from the beginning of the string and no closer to the end of the string than 4 or 5 characters away. For simplicity's sake, let's just test for a 3-character extension, which would mean 5 characters away. Here's a line that adds this test to the example function.

```
1  function validateEmail() {
2     var addressIsLegal = true;
3     var eEntered =
document.getElementById("address").value;
4     if (eEntered.indexOf(" ") !== -1) {
5        addressIsLegal = false;
6     }
7     if (eEntered.indexOf("@") < 1 ||
eEntered.indexOf("@")eEntered.length - 5) {
8        addressIsLegal = false;
9     }
10    if (addressIsLegal === false) {
11       alert("Please correct email address");
12       return false;
13    }
14 }
```

About line 7: The first part, left of the pipes, tests whether the character is at the beginning of the address, which would be illegal. The second part, right of the pipes, tests whether there are fewer than 4 characters following the character. Since there must be at least one character for the domain name plus a dot plus at least two characters for the extension, fewer than 4 characters following the @ would be illegal.

Finally, I'll add a test for the dot that needs to be at least 1 character away from the "@" and have 2 to 4 characters following it.

```
1   function validateEmail() {
2       var addressIsLegal = true;
3       var eEntered =
document.getElementById("address").value;
4       if (eEntered.indexOf(" ") !== -1) {
5           addressIsLegal = false;
6       }
7       if (eEntered.indexOf("@") < 1 || eEntered.indexOf("@")
eEntered.length - 5) {
8           addressIsLegal = false;
9       }
10      if (eEntered.indexOf(".") - eEntered.indexOf("@") < 2
|| eEntered.indexOf(".") > eEntered.length - 3) {
11          addressIsLegal = false;
12      }
13      if (addressIsLegal === false) {
14          alert("Please correct email address");
15          return false;
16      }
17  }
```

Line 10: There must be at least one character between the dot and
the *@*. The first part, left of the pipes, tests whether that one character
(or more) is missing, which would be illegal. There must also be at least
2 characters following the dot. The second part, right of the pipes, tests
whether there are fewer than 2 characters following the character,
which would be illegal.

All of the tests shown above, and more besides, can be incorporated
into a single regular expression test. A regular expression expresses a
pattern that, in this case, the user's entry must match in order to
validate. If you're familiar with the wildcard operator, *, which stands
for "any combination of characters of any length," that's the general
idea. But regular expressions go far beyond the wildcard operator.

Coding Alternatives to Be Aware Of

Regular expressions warrant a book of their own, and are beyond the
scope of this book. But, to give you a taste of how powerful (and
succinct!) they can be, here's an example. It tests for all the illegalities
that the code above checks for, and more. (This won't be covered in the
exercises for the chapter, so don't try to memorize anything in the
example.)

```
1 function validateEmail() {
2    var eEntered =
document.getElementById("address").value;3    var
emailCorrectPattern = /^[\w\-\.\+]+\@[a-zA-Z0-9\. \-]+\.[a-
zA-Z0-9]{2,4}$/;
4    if (!(eEntered.match(emailCorrectPattern))) {
5       alert("Please correct email address");
6       return false;
7    }
8 }
```

Find the interactive coding exercises for this chapter at
http://www.ASmarterWayToLearn.com/js/86.html

87
Exceptions: try and catch

If you run the following code, nothing will happen.

```
1 function greetWorld() {
2 var greeting = "Hello world!";
3 aler(greeting);
4 }
```

The keyword **alert**, misspelled **aler**, breaks the code. But JavaScript doesn't tell you what's wrong. It's like a car that won't start. Is it the battery? The fuel line? A spark plug?

Of course, in the small piece of code above, it's easy to spot the problem. But what if the function runs 40 lines and calls three other functions? It would be nice if JavaScript reported the specific problem to you instead of just breaking. Well, that's what **try...catch** is for. Here's how it works.

```
1 function greetWorld() {
2   try {
3     var greeting = "Hello world!";
4     aler(greeting);
5   }
6 catch(err) {
7     alert(err);
8   }
9 }
```

The original operational code is wrapped in the *try* block. The misformed **aler** causes a JavaScript error, which is passed to the *catch* block. An alert displays the error that caused the problem.

When you wrap some operational code in a *try* block, you say to JavaScript, "Try to execute this code. If there's an error, stop executing, and go to the *catch* block to see what to do." In the example above, the error thrown by JavaScript is assigned to the parameter **err**, and that value is displayed in an alert:

"ReferenceError: Can't find variable: aler"

Okay, so in this case JavaScript doesn't give you exactly the information you want. Instead of letting you know that you left a "t" off the **alert** keyword, it tells you it has encountered a variable that hasn't been defined. But close enough. JavaScript has pointed you in the right direction.

Note that **try** and **catch** are always paired. Without **try**, an error won't trigger **catch**. Without **catch**, JavaScript won't know what to do when it throws an error.

Some more things to keep in mind:

- The code inside the *try* and the *catch* blocks is wrapped in curly brackets.

- The functional code inside the *try* block is indented.

- The error parameter, in this case **err**, can take any legal variable name.

- In this example, an alert displays when an error occurs. But you could do something else.

The *try* and *catch* pair have limited usefulness. For example, in the example above, if you omit a parenthesis, bracket, or quotation mark, or if you have too many of them, no alert will display. The code will just break, and nothing will happen. The *try* and *catch* approach is useful mainly for spotting variables that haven't been defined or, as in this case, errors that JavaScript interprets as variables that haven't been defined.

Find the interactive coding exercises for this chapter at http://www.ASmarterWayToLearn.com/js/87.html

88
Exceptions: throw

By adding one or more *throw* statements, you can define your own errors in a *try...catch* pair. This can be useful for dealing with wayward user behavior.

Suppose you've asked the user to create a password. It must be at least 8 to 12 characters long, must contain at least one number, and can't contain any spaces. This is the markup that creates the form, simplified to keep you focused on the essentials:

```
<form onSubmit="return checkPassword();">
  Enter a password<br>
  (8-12 characters, at least 1 number, no spaces)<br>
  <input type="text" id="f1">
  <input type="submit" value="Submit">
</form>
```

This is the function that tests whether the user's input has met the requirements. If not, the function displays an alert.

```
1   function checkPassword() {
2     try {
3       var pass = document.getElementById("f1").value;
4       if (pass.length < 8) {
5           throw "Please enter at least 8 characters.";
6       }
7       if (pass.indexOf(" ") !== -1) {
8           throw "No spaces in the password, please.";
9       }
10      var numberSomewhere = false;
11      for (var i = 0; i < pass.length; i++) {
12        if (isNaN(pass(i, i+1)) === false) {
13          numberSomewhere = true;
14          break;
15        }
16      }
17      if (numberSomewhere === false) {
18          throw "Include at least 1 number.";
19      }
20    }
21    catch(err) {
22      alert(err);
23    }
24  }
```

Lines 4 through 9 and 17 through 19 test for three different user errors, with a customized string thrown for each error. The *catch* code, instead of catching a JavaScript-generated error, catches the string sent by **throw**. This is the value that is assigned to the variable **err** in line 21 and serves as the display message in line 22.

Note that any type of value, including a number or Boolean, can be passed to the catch parameter via **throw**. You can also pass a variable.

Find the interactive coding exercises for this chapter at http://www.ASmarterWayToLearn.com/js/88.html

89
Handling events within JavaScript

In earlier chapters you learned how to handle events like a button click or form submission with inline event handlers. That is the oldest and least abstract way to do it. But according to the professional coder's separate-church-and-state ethos, the functionality of JavaScript should be kept separate from the content of HTML. First, an example of the less desirable inline approach:

```
<input type="button" value="Click" onClick="sayHello();">
```

We're going to remove the highlighted part of the markup above, and we're going to add an id.

```
<input type="button" value="Click" id="button1">
```

Here's the JavaScript code that handles the event

```
1 var b1 = document.getElementById("button1");
2 b1.onclick = sayHello;
```

Line 1 assigns the element to the variable **b1**. Line 2 watches for the element to be clicked. When that happens, it calls the function **sayHello**.

Things to notice:

- Unlike the camelCase used for inline event-handling, the event name must be all-lowercase or it won't work. It's **onclick** not **onClick**, **onfocus** not **onFocus**, **onsubmit** not **onSubmit**

- Unlike inline event-handling, the function name following the equal sign isn't in quotes.

- Unlike inline event-handling, there are no parentheses following the function name.

If you wanted, you could condense it into a single statement by writing...

```
document.getElementById("button1").onclick = sayHello;
```

The function code is the same whether you use inline or scripted event-handling. For example:

```
1 function sayHello() {
2   alert("Hi there.");
3 }
```

This code calls a function that swaps one image for another when the user mouses over the original image.

```
1 var targetImg = document.getElementById("i12");
2 targetImg.onmouseover = swapPic;
```

This code calls a function that validates an email address when a form is submitted.

```
1 var emailFrm = document.getElementById("form5");
2 emailFrm.onsubmit = valEmail;
```

Find the interactive coding exercises for this chapter at http://www.ASmarterWayToLearn.com/js/89.html

Acknowledgments

If you like the book and the online exercises, gi
ve a tip of the hat to these readers, who took the time to tell me about
some things that weren't working in Version 1.0 and made other
contributions as well. This program is now so much better because of
their generosity.

Aaron Rumery

Abby Grossman

Adam Borovkoff

Al Granberg

Alan Forbes

Alan Yorinks

Alex Jones

Allie Etcoff

Allison Burns

Andrew Bowers

Andrew Brassington

Andrew Mayne at
http://andrewmayn
e.com

Andy Schwartz

Anne Messenger

Axel Estborn

Bashir Aziz

Ben O'Loghlin

Bettina Bergren

Bill Sterner

Blaise Gratton

Bob Cochran

Bob Rand

Boris Đemrovski|

Brad Mellema

Brenan Morisset

Brent Lee

Brian Eggert

Brian Maurer

Brian Sheets

Callum Makkai

Cameron Arndt

Casey McCann

Cesar De La Cruz

Charlie Davis

Chaz Hirales

Chris Heinze

Chris Horne

Christopher Griffin

Christopher Urrutia

Clyde Eugene
Makamure

Craig Berthiaume

Dan Perata

Dan Shafer

Danial Ghani

Daniel Albornoz

Daryl Martin

Dave Murley

Dave Persinger

David Clark

David Gould

David White

Dean Bunnell

Dennis Hudson

Derek

Diana Monroy

Don Platt

Dorian Maiga

Douglas Corin

Douglas Goode

Eric Brengle

Eric Carraway

Eric Smith

Erkki Majamaki

Estevan Maito

Francesco Badraun

Frank Shen

Gary Polofka

Gene Kraybill

George Schweitzer

GJ Griffiths's friend

Glenn Cole

Gordon Baker

Huilin Chen

Igor Arsenkin

IK Song

Ivan Dimov

Ivan Nikolov

Jack McKinnon

Jacob Turner

James Pieper

James Foxworthy

Jaroslaw
Olewniczak

Jason Bray

Jay Vics

Jeff Bauer

Jeff Santos

Jennifer Bland

Jeremy Williams

Joel Kohlbusch

John Koch

John Luko

John Veld

Jon Seidel

Jon W.
Christopherson

Jonah Koch

Jordan Ball

Jordan Diez

Jordan Kimball

Justin Mckenney

Justin Sparks

Kamil Baran

Keith Grout

Kenneth Wells

Kent Searight

Kevin Gigiano at
http://kevgig.com/

Kim Leung

Kiran Bedi

Laine Gebhardt

Lane Watson

Laura Kirchner

Lauren Zugai

Lawrence Kennon

Lee Sarrasin

Lene Nytoft Laursen

Leno Lewis

Leon Robert
Walpole

Lester Colegado

Lino Jimenez

Luke Lancaster

Manzo

Mary Cooke

Marie Lee
Mark Wilhelm
Martin Andrews
Mary Ann Howell
Mary Elizabeth
Mathew Mitchell
Matt Elliott
Matt Jared
Matt Kolat
Matthew Highland
Maurice Andre
Megan Stetz
Michael Crayne
Michael Williams
Mike Armishaw
Mike Griffin
Morgan Atwood
Mukesh Kumar
Natalie Akam
Nate Snyder
Neil Chudgar
Nick Green
Nikov Sieber
Nils-Gunnar
Nilsson
Osvaldo Dias dos
Santos
Øyvind Mo
Paul Hume
Peter Moulding
Peter Rihn
Phillip Chan
Quint Rahaman
Rafael Oliveira
Richard Korgan
Rick Norris
Robert Hecht
Robert Johnson
Robert Newhart
Ross Updegraff
Russ Thornton
Ryan Smith

Santosh Walvekar
Scott Smeester
Sean Herrala
Seth Spearman
Shang
Sharina Jones
Silvia Angelov
Simon Harms at
http://www.simonharm s.com
Srinath Kameswaran
Steve Jazic
Steve Medwin
Steven Noe
Steven Rueter
Syad Ali Raza
Thomas Mechau
Tim Miller
Tim Poppe
Tino Allen
Tom Boyles
Tom Gough
Tom Johnson
Tomas Sandala
Tris Nefzger
Umesh Berry
Unnat Jain
Uriel Cota
Vijay Luthra
Vinod Nair
Wenying Piao
William MacCorkell
William Thompson

Index

d

Made in the USA
Middletown, DE
31 January 2018